MEDITATION CHALLENGE

90 DAY MEDITATION CHALLENGE

How to Build a Daily Mindfulness Practice

By
Tim Ebl and Kyla Dagenais

Copyright © 2019 Tim Ebl and Kyla Dagenais
All rights reserved.

Publishing Services by Happy Self Publishing
www.happyselfpublishing.com

Year: 2019

All rights reserved. No reproduction, transmission or copy of this publication can be made without the written consent of the author in accordance with the provision of the Copyright Acts. Any person doing so will be liable to civil claims and criminal prosecution.

Happy Self Publishing.

DISCLAIMER

This book is intended to help readers build a healthy lifestyle habit of meditation, that will deepen their life experience while making the world a better place for everyone.

It is not intended to replace the guidance of an experienced teacher or mentor. Please seek the assistance of a teacher to help you on your path.

It is not intended to replace the care of your regular family physician or any other medical professional. If you have a history of mental illness, addiction to substances, are using medications or substances which alter perceptions or moods, history of seizures or epilepsy, or unexplained medical lapses, or any other mental issues which require medical attention and/ or intervention/ and/ or medication, we ask that you consult your family doctor before beginning any meditation practice.

If you encounter any strange side effects from meditation, such as dizziness or altered mental states, or any other unusual events, please consult a medical professional immediately.

If you have emotional issues that you prefer to leave buried under layers of mental business, be advised that mindfulness and meditation may cause you to face these issues and deal with them. If this isn't something you are prepared for, please stop here!

*This book reviews some of the commonly accepted benefits of meditation that have been reported on and studied by others. We make no promises or claims that using this book will have the same benefits or effects for our readers. But if you do **start levitating** or gain **extra sensory perception**, or any other fantastic abilities (such as **Super Smelling** or **Smile Projection**), then we accept full responsibility for giving you superpowers. Please send your video or photo with proof so we can brag about your accomplishments that are in this case directly caused by us!*

Thanks for joining us! We are so glad you decided to read our book that we want to thank you with a free gift!

You might be thinking, and how am I going to get this so-called free gift, you're thousands of miles away? And not that long ago, you would be correct. A reader would have to endure the unthinkable agony and inconvenience of sending their address by snail-mail to us. Then they would have to wait while we got the scribe monk at the old scriptorium to laboriously copy the document onto vellum, package it, and snail-mail it to you. It used to really try one's patience. But, since we no longer live in those times, we went a different way. Using cutting edge technology, we digitized this gift so we can just send it straight to you.

This is a special offer to all of our readers. We want you to have two things- a downloadable, printable calendar and a 90-Day Meditation Challenge Guide to help you make the most of this journey.

All you need to do if you decide to grab this free gift is go to www.tim-ebl.com/bonus, and we will get it straight to you.

The calendar is designed to make it easy to keep track of the 90 days, and it's easily printable so you can put it in your day-timer, hang it on the wall, put it on the fridge, etc. It's editable so you can customize it to fit your needs as well.

The guide will be a handy reference for you so you can easily double check what the next step is. There are some quick tips and reminders to refer to, to help you keep on track. It has space for notes, so you can jot things down if you like. This feature will be super handy for anyone that is reading this as an eBook - you won't have the paper copy to refer to, so you can use our 90-day Meditation Challenge Guide. There are some quick tips and reminders in the guide to refer to, to keep you on track.

So if these free items would be useful to you, please go to www.tim-ebl.com and get them!

Don't want to get this stuff yet? Don't worry, we will be mentioning them a few more times just to make sure you don't forget about them. That's because we really, really, really want you to have them to make this the best possible experience that you can have. And we spent a lot of time setting up a website, making the gifts, then running them through the digitizer repeatedly until we got the darn thing to work. After all that effort, we really need a few people to go get this stuff, so we don't feel bad.

This book is dedicated to the cause of inner peace

And the force of love.

For those who came before us to light the way

And those who will come after to forge new trail.

MORE BY THE AUTHORS

Demons in the Cellar, by Tim Ebl

Books in the works:

-Self Talk Tips, Tricks and Tactics, by Tim Ebl

TABLE OF CONTENTS

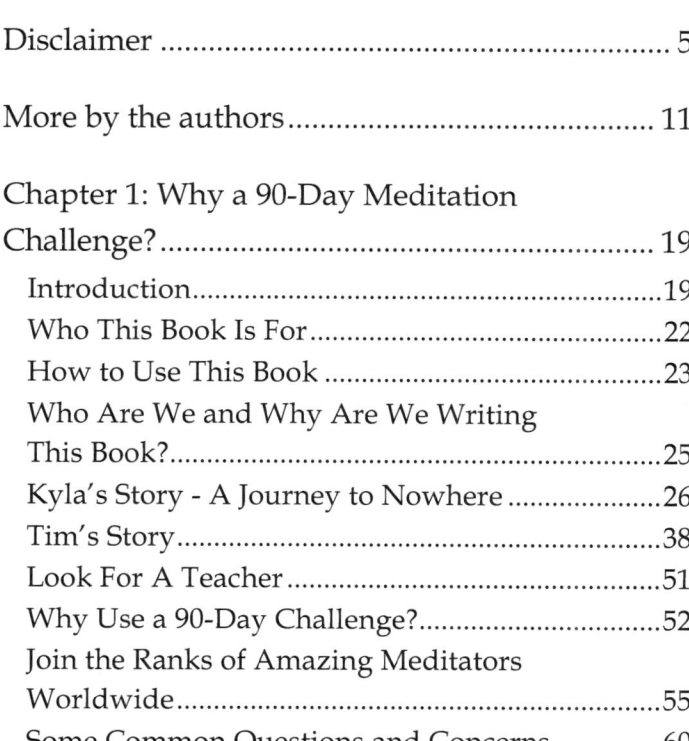

Disclaimer	5
More by the authors	11
Chapter 1: Why a 90-Day Meditation Challenge?	19
Introduction	19
Who This Book Is For	22
How to Use This Book	23
Who Are We and Why Are We Writing This Book?	25
Kyla's Story - A Journey to Nowhere	26
Tim's Story	38
Look For A Teacher	51
Why Use a 90-Day Challenge?	52
Join the Ranks of Amazing Meditators Worldwide	55
Some Common Questions and Concerns	60

Start Now! Day 1 64
This Chapter's Key Takeaway Points: 67

Chapter 2: Meditation is Good for You! 69
History of Meditation - A Very Brief Recounting .. 69
Why Do We Want to Meditate? 72
Health Benefits 76
Effects of Meditation on the Mind 83
Meditation and Mindfulness Can Dilate Time 87
Key Takeaway Points From chapter 2 90

Chapter 3: How The Heck Do We Do This Meditation Thing? 93
The Basics 93
Setting For Sitting: The Sitting Setting 96
Meditation Altar or Shrines 98
Distractions 100
Kyla's Viewpoint on Distractions: 104
Timing 107
Getting Your Body Ready For Meditation 113
Mental Prep 113
Positive Reinforcement To Build Commitment .. 116
What To Do If You Miss A Day (Or Two) 119
Want to Build a Daily Practice? Don't Let Yourself Make Excuses 122
Habit Creation Lock-In Master Tricks That You Really Need To Use! 124
Key Takeaway Points From chapter 3 127

Chapter 4: The 90-Day Schedule! 131

What If I Want To Meditate Longer? 131
I Want To Use A different Meditation That
I Know Of. Can I Still Do The Challenge? 132
Days 1 to 10 133
Days 11 to 20 136
Days 21 to 30 138
Days 31 to 40 138
Days 41 to 50 140
Days 51 to 60 141
Days 61 to 70 143
Days 71 to 80 144
Days 81 to 90 144
Finish Line - Celebrate! 145
Key Takeaway Points From chapter 4 146

Chapter 5: Using a Calendar 149

The Streak Method 150
Paper Calendars 153
Journal 154
Smartphone Apps 156
Our Custom Calendar 157
Key Takeaway Points From Chapter 5 158

Chapter 6: Support System 161

How to Succeed - Part of a Team 161
Family or Friends 162
Buddy System 163
Facebook Page 164

Website 164
Key Takeaway Points From Chapter 6 165

Chapter 7: The Body and Meditation 167
The Yoga Connection 167
Kyla's Body Awareness and Tension
Relieving Breath Primer 168
Tension in the Face, Neck, and Shoulders
Reduces Brain Capacity! 171
Releasing the Spine 172
Releasing Tension in the Hips and Legs 172
Breathing, You're Already a Winner! 173
From Head to Toe or Toe to Head 174
Releasing Tension for Those With Limited
Mobility 179

Chapter 8: Alternative Meditations and Systems, and Finding a Teacher 183
Why You Should Consider A Teacher and
Further Training 183
Alternative Meditations 185
Object Focused Meditation 186
Visualization 187
Mantras 190
Walking Meditation 192
Transcendental Meditation 195
Loving Kindness Meditation 196
Key Takeaway Points From Chapter 8 198

Chapter 9: Where to Go From Here 201
- Keep Up The Practice! 201
- Joining a Monastery 202
- Workshops, Courses, and Local Meditation Groups 204
- Meditation Retreats 205
- Set Up Your Own Mini-Meditation Retreat 209
- Kyla's Silent Retreat Experience 213
- Great Books That Can Help Your Practice 215
- Resources 217
- Key Takeaway Points From Chapter 9 218

Chapter 10: Conclusion 221
- What we Hope For You 221

Acknowledgments 227

CHAPTER 1

WHY A 90-DAY MEDITATION CHALLENGE?

Introduction

"Meditation is something I really want to do - but I don't know where to start!"

"How do you know if you are meditating or if you are just sitting there?"

"I always fall asleep when I try."

"I tried a few times over the years, but I just didn't keep at it - now it feels like I really missed the boat."

We've talked to a lot of people about meditation, and these are just a few of the things we've heard. Some are interested in meditation and mindfulness, they want to try it, but they just can't seem to find a way to get started. Maybe they feel that they don't have time. Maybe they are afraid that they won't be able to do it right. Maybe they don't think they can find a quiet enough place to really "concentrate."

Meditation and mindfulness have so many benefits that it's impossible to cover them in just this one book! Study after study show that meditation can result in reduced stress levels, increased creativity, increased happiness, better immune system responses, lowered blood pressure, better sex, and maybe even fewer speeding tickets. It can help with insomnia, anxiety, and worry. It can put you in touch with your soul and let you focus on your spiritual side. It's obvious why so many people want to start meditating. But for some, it's just so hard to get going! How can you get on the cushion and see what it's all about?

This is what we want to help you with. We want to get you started on a lifelong habit that will change your life. Kyla, a yoga instructor and meditation teacher with years of experience, has practical knowledge and tips to get your show on the road. And Tim, an author, licensed Heartmath Certified Coach, yoga enthusiast, and construction worker, has a unique view of how mindfulness can impact lives. Together, we believe that we can coach you through a 90-day challenge and watch you coast off into the distance.

Meditation really can help you to live with less stress. It really can lead to a healthier body and a more creative mindset. Meditating daily can improve every single one of your personal interactions. And meditation really can help you get fewer speeding tickets! (Hint: it has to do with increased patience.)

Later, in the next chapter, we will go over exactly how meditation can do all this. There is scientific proof and everything. And if science isn't enough for you, we have the subjective, anecdotal experiences we ourselves can offer.

Here is our promise to you. Start on this journey with us, and you will live a richer, deeper life. Meditate with us for 90 days, and you will be calmer, have less anxiety, have more energy, more self-control, and a little more space in your head. The small amount of time you will spend reading this book and sitting still each day will pay you back in huge ways. We guarantee it!

With this kind of return on your investment, we urge you to start this journey and not stop for anything. Don't just read the book and then put it aside. Take the challenge.

Meditating is nearly free. The benefits are amazing. There is no time like now to get started. So, what are you waiting for? Let's get to the good stuff!

Who This Book Is For

This book is for anyone that wants to start meditation practice, or has meditated, but didn't know if they were doing it right, or anyone who just wants to start meditating every day but hasn't been able to get themselves to do it. We will cover a lot of real hard evidence of the benefits of meditation, as well as the tiniest bit of history <shudder>. That means this book is also for anyone who wants to know more about the science and the reasons for wanting mindfulness in your life. This book is for all positive humans who want to learn and grow!

This book is for people who can spare a few minutes a day to do some much-needed self-care, to recover from the stressful outside world and clear your thoughts.

And finally, this book is for everyone with a sense of humor. Meditation isn't all about stiff-necked, serious, and solemn monks who punish themselves by whacking their foreheads with large tomes. Meditation doesn't mean taking yourself too seriously. We are going to try and have some fun with it.

How to Use This Book

Have you ever read about how to do something, been really excited about the new knowledge, and after finishing the book, pretty much forgotten all of the details? This is definitely a thing that has happened to us. But what can you do to lock it in?

One thing that you could do would be to use a highlighter on all the parts you find the most important, and then go back and reread them, or take some notes as you go through. If this is an electronic copy, please use the highlighter function instead of an actual highlighter on your screen!

Repetition is the key. If you read over the information more than once, you will remember it when you need it. This also helps to remind you and motivate you to do the thing!

If you download the free 90-Day Meditation guide at www.tim-ebl.com, some of the most important tips and information will be handy for you to refer to later, to refresh your memory.

Who Are We and Why Are We Writing This Book?

We wanted to give you a bit of an inside look on why we decided to write this book. Who are Kyla and Tim, why do they think meditation is so important, and why should they be telling us about it? What challenges did they meet, how did they overcome them, and what did they learn that can help others avoid the pitfalls? Or at least learn to sit through them...

> *Meditation practice isn't about trying to throw ourselves away and become better, it's about befriending who you are."*
> *-Ani Pema Chodron*

We feel our stories are important because they show that meditation isn't just some airy-fairy, cushion-sitting way to waste time. It has huge effects on your mental and spiritual development, true. It also has actual real-world applications, from assisting physical healing to better work performance.

Kyla's Story - A Journey to Nowhere

Who are you, Kyla? What makes you an expert? Nothing but the time spent through practice and teaching. Even in teaching, I am the student. As people come to me, each is very different in their understanding of life, and it's my job to hold space for them to find their own path to peace, to help them access the unique recipe for their minds to soften. Hundreds of students later, it is them that have shaped and developed me as a teacher. I've often questioned, who is really teaching who? They arrive with specific problems or a desire to meditate to create many different outcomes in their lives. Some wishing to cultivate more abundance of peace, love, money, gratitude. All wanting to let go of what holds them back from their highest potential. People wishing to escape the traps they have created for themselves in their minds.

Over the past seven years, teaching has taken many different shapes. My students and I have navigated many different blocks and patterns. Some of us have been together for years, and others have only needed one or two appointments to set out on their way of deeper self-awareness. I never really advertised and am able to work full time teaching yoga and meditation by word of mouth, mostly on a private basis. I accept that this is my purpose here, it is what I was born to do. I continually feel grateful to witness people's arrival to themselves. To hear them breathe into this moment in full acceptance of what is. I am grateful to every person I have had the pleasure of sitting with, as they have taught me more in their quest then they will ever know.

My meditation journey began very early, as a 14-year-old girl growing up in a small rural Canadian town. At my first group meditation, Ron spoke of things I had never heard of, things like alternate dimensions and life beyond humanity. I was so intrigued by his words and ideas, that I knew I had to look deeper. From that moment forward, I wanted to understand perception and consciousness. I wanted to know why each of us was so different, and ultimately: Why am I here? What is this life? I began my quest for self-realization. Armed with my photocopied handout of the meditation we did that night, I would read from the sheet and follow the instructions.

I devoured as many books as I could find on the mind and its functions, on reality and perspective of hypnosis and meditation. I became fascinated by hypnosis and the psychology greats, how we function together as a society and separately as individuals. I began to experiment with my own subconscious. I would try to hypnotize my friends and family, mostly using my new-found skills for party tricks. I was introduced to a hypnotist, and we began to hang out. I wanted to learn as much as I could from this person and would attend group sessions as often as I could. It was during one of these sessions that I kept hearing the message, "get your head checked." I ignored the message as just the ramblings of the mind.

One morning I woke up with limited sight in my right eye. Being a teenager, I thought that it was maybe caused by the makeup I had on when I went to bed the night before. Days passed, and still blurred vision. I asked my mom to take me to the optometrist in the city, and she did. The optometrist took one look in my eye and with zero hesitation told me I needed to go to Vancouver for further assessment. The prognosis: brain tumor.

The doctors did not understand the tumor that had developed in my brain and surrounded my optic nerve. This type of tumor was typically found in small children and had only surfaced in my body as a young teen. I was subjected to many, many tests, some of them extraordinarily painful. I would prepare myself with meditation, using the skills I had acquired during my studies. It gave me somewhere to go amidst the pain. The tests and medication intervention went on for almost a year until a doctor from Chicago became interested in my case. Once transferred to his care, we decided that the medication was only making me sick, and I chose to have a biopsy. The medical experts had been trying to avoid this, since once you touch the optic nerve, the damage is irreversible. Up until this point, they had been trying to shrink the tumor with medication to avoid permanent damage. I was very tired at this point and no longer wanted what I perceived to be poison in my body, and I opted for the surgery, with the direction that they were not to dig into my brain. They were only to remove the part of the tumor on the nerve itself. I had full understanding that I would become completely blind in my right eye, but at that point in time, I did not understand how becoming half blind would affect my life and the way I would move in it.

The surgery went well, and I was released after a week. I then began my new life. I had made the choice to enjoy a life of quality over quantity. I chose to forgo any medication and would approach the reins of the tumor with eating well, laughter therapy, and meditation. I just couldn't do the medication anymore.

It took three years and four MRIs to confirm, but I finally received the call that I had been waiting for. Beyond the understanding of my doctors, the brain tumor was gone.

I was still struggling to live without depth perception and how much my right eye had meant to me and my ability to function in society. I would reach for something and would miss it completely. I would be trying to cook and miss the pan or put my hand right on it. I would run into people and things on a regular basis. And, forget trying to walk on uneven surfaces!

I had always been sensitive, but becoming blind in one eye brought things to a whole new level. It is so very true that when you lose a sense, the others become stronger. Echos would disorient me, and I could hear the hum of fluorescent lights very clearly. Things became chaotic, and for a while, I forgot all about meditation. I grew fearful and reclusive. I was not offered any sort of rehabilitation and had begun to think that it was me, that I was going crazy. I wanted to go to college to formally study the psychology greats that I had read about in my teens, but the thought of all the sounds and crowded halls paralyzed me.

I found solace in meditation; if I could stay mindful, my ability to navigate the world was much easier. It was off to college I went.

Two years into my studies, I became pregnant with my first son, and my focus shifted once again. My pregnancy was turbulent, and it was questionable if the baby would arrive at all. About to become a new mother, I was on a new journey of study.

Meditation and childbirth. Meditation for pain. Meditation for healing ill babies in utero.

After all this, life had been kind enough to offer me true understanding of mind over matter. My pregnancy went full term, and when it came time to welcome my new son to the world, meditation had prepared me so well, I was able to deliver my new love without medication or making a sound. Meditation for the win once again.

I wish I could say that it was smooth sailing from there. I wish I could tell you that I no longer would suffer from bouts of anxiety and depression. The truth is, after my son arrived, I was so preoccupied with trying to keep him alive that my meditation practice slipped into the background. Without these mental resets, anxiety and depression became overwhelming, and my home life was not so healthy. The months after the birth of my son would be some of the hardest months of my life to date.

My parents chose to separate. I lost both my great grandmas and a cousin that was partially raised in my family home, I considered him more of a brother, as I was eight years older and had been heavily involved in his growth and development. The nature of his passing was dark and shameful.

I found out that my then-husband had been having an affair, and I knew I would be facing the world as a single mother. The depression and anxiety became overwhelming. Perhaps it was all the shame, maybe it was the fear of not being able to provide well for my son. I felt alone. I felt defeated, and I could not bring myself to sit in meditation. I could not bring myself to any point of self-care. I did not feel deserving of any sort of love, especially my son's. Dark days were upon me.

I began to drink heavily on the seven days I did not have my son. Being raised around alcoholism, from the beginning of motherhood, I knew this is not what I had wanted for my life, and especially for my beautiful son. I noticed it was becoming harder and harder to not drink on the week he was supposed to be with me.

As always, I was reading. I happened to be working on a book by the Dalai Lama. He made reference to yogis, the effects of yoga, and the ability to deepen meditation. I signed up for the next yoga class I could find.

It took place on Saturday mornings. I knew that if I committed to this for eight weeks, I would not go out on drinking on Friday as I had to be in class Saturday morning. Outsmarting myself, the plan worked.

My first experience with yoga was brutal. I felt so weak, and it was clear that it was both in mind and body. My limbs would shake, and most of the poses were impossible to perform. I kept going.

Over the course of eight weeks, I noticed my body and mind both grow in strength. I was hooked. As learning any new skill goes, I wasn't entirely sure why I was responding in this way. At the time, I had no idea of the internal benefits that were taking place, I just felt better. It was easier to move in my body, and the frantic times of panic seemed to reduce, becoming fewer and fewer. I was able to meditate just a little deeper. I continued to pick up a yoga class here and there, and I remember very clearly one day sitting in a class and looking at the teacher thinking, "my goodness, how lucky to be a yoga teacher." Little did I know about what the universe had in store for me.

It would be a couple of years and another beautiful baby boy until I would be sitting in front of a computer trying to decide what I would like to do with my life. I googled yoga teacher training, and there it was. Prana Yoga College. For the first time in my life, I took what it was that I truly wanted. I booked my trip to Bali, Indonesia and began what would turn out to be my life's purpose. I was introduced to Shakti Mhi and Joseph Pepe Danza, but most importantly, my breath.

What had been missing from my yoga practice from the beginning was the ability to create internal space and alignment from the inside. It was the ability to not force but accept and to release into the yoga pose. The world of yoga and meditation opened to me in a way that made all the difference. Until that point, I had been taught to force things into alignment. I had been shown to look at myself from the outside, to want to "look" just like everyone else in the class, and to judge my yoga by the shape of my body.

Shakti offered me respite in the seat of my soul, she offered me acceptance of self and acceptance for my journey, she offered me... Me. In all my faults and glory, she offered me the ability to rise above my mind and introduced me to my breath.

It has been seven years since then, and I have not once lost the peace of my breath. Don't get me wrong, I've lost my center many times. But my ability to breathe and find home within stayed.

My life's work is to offer this gift to others. Many students have come and gone, each with a different story, a different reason, a different wanting, and the application has been the same. The breath and acceptance, together, we work to find what brings peace to their minds and bodies. Eventually, we are able to rest and let go, entirely in this moment. We find a way together to this moment right now, beyond the mind's ramblings, beyond the patterns of thought. We rest fully in the breath, fully in the moment.

To be honest with you, I don't know if I will ever reach the space of mastery, and for me as a yogi, that means to exist in a space of continuous meditation. I am 18 years + into my practice, and I still at times lose my breath and get wrapped up in my ego. Mastery is not something that I would ever claim, as I do not know what is around the corner on this life adventure, and I feel as soon as I would make a claim as such, life would give me a situation to test my said mastery. It feels better for me to just allow and accept each breath as it comes, and when it gets lost, I personally use the techniques that I teach. I am, in the end, a student of life and meditation, seeking the waves of breath just like everyone else. Just with many years invested.

It has been countless classes and hundreds of students since then. Each person is unique, as is practice. Each with a particular path ...h life, but all having one thing in common. The breath leads them home. The breath leads them past the safety of mind and into the seat of their heart. It is this that meditation offers, and it is this hope that I offer the readers of this book: a way to their hearts. Wherever this journey leads you, dear reader, I hope it is to inner peace and self-acceptance, which everyone deserves. For more information on my work, retreats or online classes check out: www.intothewildwithkyla.com

With love,
Kyla

Tim's Story

I've always been interested in meditation. I've experimented with everything from affirmations to guided visualization, to breathwork, to self-hypnosis. I eventually settled into my current daily habit of 20 to 60 minutes of mindful breath awareness in the morning and 20 minutes of a loving-kindness meditation at night.

I'm also a licensed Heartmath Certified Coach. Heartmath training and technology improves emotional resilience and reduces stress with breathing exercises and utilizes a biofeedback device that can connect to your smartphone or computer. Using the Inner Balance App and sensor, you can track your heart rate variability. While this isn't a traditional meditation, it can be a helpful addition to a traditional practice. For more information on this technology, check out www.tim-ebl.com or www.heartmath.com.

What I find most people struggle with, is how to begin their meditation journey and turn it into daily practice. Well, I've done a lot of the groundwork for you. I've researched and experimented with habit formation and tricks to get myself to do things for years now. While every single one of these hacks I've collected won't work for everyone, some of them will. I know this because I am one of the laziest people out there. So, I've been forced to learn all these ways to influence myself, just to get anything done! I use these same tactics to write daily, get in my yoga practice, and to meditate. None of them are rocket surgery; they can be applied by anyone!

I've found that relying on willpower and motivation doesn't work at all for me. I needed to build a better mousetrap (or humantrap) and then place it in my way. Does it sound gimmicky to use tips, tricks, and hacks to learn how to meditate? Personally, I feel the results are the important thing. If we can follow the right steps to just get sitting on that cushion, then we have achieved the goal. The thing is to build a system to help us along.

Let's take a quick look at how meditation has affected my life, and why I really want to help you get the same benefits for yourself. There's a ton more to this story, but I'll stick to how my journey has helped me get meditating consistently, and how this can help you too.

I am a construction guy with a background of working with my hands and building things. I work in an industry that is based on short-term jobs working away from home for weeks at a time. The shifts are long, with 10 or 12-hour days being common. Living conditions are stressful, usually staying in a work camp at remote locations with hundreds of other dudes that I don't know, all in close proximity.

The actual work is demanding, with manual lifting, stairs and ladders, noisy and dusty environments. There can be a lot of pressure to meet deadlines. Many of my coworkers are stressed from all the same things I just mentioned, and there is the potential for interpersonal "breakdowns" at any moment. Also, substance abuse is pretty common in this kind of construction job. To top it all off, you never know when you will be laid off due to the project coming close to the end, or work shortages, or lack of funds left in the budget. The fear levels can run high when everyone is worried about how they will get paychecks and support their families. In short, I spent a lot of time in a very stressful environment, far from home.

Being apart from my wife and kids was stressful too. When you don't have the home environment to sink into every day, you are missing the basic emotional support system that so many people completely take for granted. And your family at home is stressed from you not being there. This leads to feelings of guilt or being cheated out of life and happiness. Large numbers of workers, mostly men, are out there working in situations very similar to what I have just described, and they feel trapped by these circumstances. They feel that their lives are out of their control, and they feel that no one understands how they feel.

The effects of my environment and all the rest of my built-in stresses and programming were that I was a very reactive person. If you pushed me, I pushed back. It was easy to use anger and force to try to solve interpersonal issues. While I got along with almost everyone, I was quick to resort to emotional violence when there seemed no other option.

I still work in this industry, and as I type these words, I'm 600+ kilometers from my home.

Now I know some will say "If it's so rough, why don't you just quit and get a different job?" My answer to this is, I'm not complaining about my circumstances, just setting the stage for you. We all make choices in life, and my choices are the exact right ones for me to learn what I needed to learn.

The majority of this time, I had an on again, off again approach to meditation that really didn't give me the results I was looking for or seem to "go anywhere." I was spinning my wheels, never really making any lasting changes in my mind. I'm sure none of this was a waste, no effort spent on yourself is a waste. As the months went on, I started looking into meditation more seriously.

I started trying various forms of sitting meditation, usually counting breaths or repeating "rise" on an inhale and "fall" on an exhale. I would time myself and go for 15-minute sessions. This seemed very calming and was more along the lines of what I needed. The problem came in not building a good habit and keeping it up; I would trail off time and again as life got in the way. A few days or weeks later, I would realize that I had totally lost track of my meditation habit. I always felt guilty and almost ashamed that I couldn't keep going with it because I really thought I was missing out on the benefits of meditation. I didn't know how true this was.

This cycle repeated for a few years. I would read about meditation, get all excited about it, and be determined to give it a try. Sometimes the book would be so long and trail off into boring explanations, with the author stretching it out just to get a high word count, that I wouldn't even be able to finish the book and get to the instructions. My brain would power out, and I would lose momentum. (This is why we are asking you to start right away! At the end of this chapter, look for the "**Start Now! Day 1**" instructions and get this ball rolling!)

So, what changed? I decided to commit to a certain time period and meditate every day, 3 times a day for 10 minutes. It was a simple meditation, with the goal being to pay attention to each breath and make the inhalation the same length as the exhalation while maintaining a feeling of positivity. It was challenging to pull off at first, but I kept at it, sometimes with success and sometimes not. It didn't seem to matter how well I followed the steps; what was more important was showing up.

I knew I couldn't just rely on willpower and motivation to keep going. Motivation always fades, and willpower can run out. I researched a lot of habit-forming techniques at this point, and as I applied what I learned, it became easier every day to show up for myself.

I found myself becoming calmer and more alert during the workday. Issues that seemed so hard to deal with before were easier to step back from and think about rationally. Gradually, day by day, my confidence and calmness increased. And gradually, day by day, I was wearing out my hip muscles and knees.

I had the idea in my head that to do this right, I needed to be sitting cross-legged for it to be a "real" meditation. The problem with this was, being a little out of shape in that area, my hips and knees just couldn't handle it. After a couple of weeks, I was having trouble walking due to sitting too long in a position that my body didn't like. I was forced to swallow my pride and sit in a chair to meditate. This turned out to work just fine. A part of me considered it a failure that I wasn't able to meditate like a "real meditator" would. Eventually, I healed back up again and was able to walk like a "real construction worker" again. The moral of this little story is that you don't need to sit in a fancy position to meditate! Maybe your body just can't do it without getting injured. At that time, I certainly couldn't sit cross-legged for meditation practice for many days in a row. And let's just say that the lotus position isn't happening for me any time soon. However, I realized this was just a distraction.

After about three months, others started noticing the change and mentioned how calm I stayed during work challenges. My direct supervisor once went with me to an extremely stressful meeting with an unreasonable client where they repeatedly tried to bully me and used personal attacks to get me to take the blame for things that were totally out of our control as a contractor. It was an "emotionally-charged" and insulting meeting! I managed to stay calm and reply with facts, instead of reacting the way I once would have. When we finally got out of the boardroom and were walking through the parking lot, my supervisor told me that he was impressed with how I handled a really difficult situation so well, and he wanted to know what I'd been doing!

Over that entire period of my life, it seemed as if the universe was lining up little challenges at work, just to see if it could get me to flinch. They didn't all go perfectly, but they went a lot better than they would have even six months before. I started to see how I could work around the things that happen to me and choose the reaction.

These changes didn't make my life all unicorns and cotton candy, that's not what I'm saying at all. What did happen is my sense of calm, self-assurance, and resilience increased. It was like I gained some sort of superpower. I could get outside myself and see what was going on with others, and it helped me to not take things personally. This might be the compassion that the gurus all talk about gaining from meditation. It's amazing how much use it is in a real-world scenario like construction, where keeping a clear head and eliminating knee-jerk reactions is a huge asset. It also helped me to guide those working under me more skillfully.

Then I let the whole thing slide for a few months again. I just stopped meditating around Christmas time, when my routine was broken up by the holidays. I took a few days off, which became many days, then months. I forgot about my practice and went unconscious again. There wasn't an immediate change, but slowly, the stresses built back up and started surfacing.

I never reverted to my original state. I still had the calmness and the ability to see beyond my own needs to understand where others were coming from, but I was feeling as if I were missing out. The world went from a place of bright colors and hope to one that was darker, more grayish. I started feeling a little depressed. I knew I needed to get my mojo back. But I couldn't get going right away, I'd lost all my momentum and didn't know where to start. This was when I listened to the audiobook "Success Through Stillness" by Russell Simmons and Chris Morrow.

This amazing book reminded me of all the benefits that meditation had to offer. The author listed all the ways meditation and stillness have helped him become a successful and happy person. It also had a simple meditation practice to follow, utilizing a mantra and 20-minute sessions twice a day. It gave me the ambition and direction to start again.

This time, there was no stopping me. I started right back in where I'd left off. It was less than a week before I felt like I'd found my forever home, inside my own head. Every meditation was different, but they all ended with a deep sense of peace that I'd never felt before. As time went on and the days added up, I started to really look forward to that feeling. So even on days where I really didn't want to sit, **I did it anyway,** because I knew how much I needed that feeling of stillness inside.

Just so you don't think I'm bragging about how wonderful and calm I always am now, you can rest assured that I'm not the most amazing and well-adjusted person on the planet. A quick talk with my wife and family will set you (and me) straight! I especially have difficulty when I'm in a long lineup at a cashier or near clowns of any sort, or around angry bees. But I am more able to see my shortcomings/programming and not always act on their faulty instructions. I have added a moment to think and maybe to choose my actions. It makes an amazing difference to how things go down. I feel like maybe I can live and let clowns and bees live, too.

I want everyone on earth to feel that they are enough, that sense of self-love, that feeling of compassion for others. I want to feel it stronger myself. I want to share this with the world! And this feeling is, for me, a direct result of meditating every day.

I want everyone to be present in their lives, and enjoy knowing others more deeply, and be able to spend what seems like more time loving their kids, helping their neighbors, enjoying a trip to the beach. I want life to be rich and full for everyone!

Look For A Teacher

We will be going into some introductory methods for meditation. This book is intended to promote meditation and help people to motivate themselves to make positive life changes. It isn't meant to replace one-on-one teaching and experienced meditation coaches. You can use our simple techniques to get you started, but to grow beyond a certain point, all skills benefit from the expert guidance of a mentor. If you think about the difference between going into a gym and just randomly lifting some weights based on a book you read or getting the assistance of a good personal trainer, there is going to be a huge difference. Yes, some people can learn a lot from a book. Others need more interaction to get where they want to be with a skill.

If books are the main way you will be learning about meditation, we have a starter pack of books for you to check out after you finish this one. We will include the titles that we used along the way and some of the most inspirational authors that have helped thousands on this journey.

Why Use a 90-Day Challenge?

> *"To earn the trust of your meditation, you have to visit it every day. It's like having a puppy."*
> *- Chelsea Richer*

What is so significant about 90 days? It sounds like a long time... But we didn't pick this number at random, there's science backing it up.

Common knowledge tells us that it takes 21 days to make or break a habit. But is this actually true or just a myth that floats around out there? It turns out that 21 days may be enough for some people and for some habits, but the average is more likely 66 days.

At University College London, Phillippa Lally worked on a study in Health Psychology that was published in the European Journal of Social Psychology in July 2009. They studied the habits of 6 people over 12 weeks to determine how long it took common new habits to become automatic. They found that, on average, it took 66 days to form a habit, which is three times longer than most people think.

Here's some good news that was also published in this study. They concluded that "missing one opportunity to perform the behavior did not materially affect the habit formation process." So if you miss one day, just keep on keeping on and pick up where you left off the next day.

90 days is long enough to rewire your brain and start to see results from your meditation. It might only take 21 days to begin forming a habit for some, but it will most likely take 66 to 90 days to make it stick and create a new lifestyle.

Another benefit to a longer challenge will be that we have the time to slowly work our way into it, not going too hardcore right off the bat. Some programs would have you jump straight in and sit for 20 minutes twice a day. This just won't work for a lot of people, and you'll end up quitting in frustration before you ever get close to feeling benefits. We don't want that. We want a slow, steady progression without overtaxing the willpower. With a 90-day window, we can start with five minutes and move toward more time as you feel you can handle it. We want to break change down into consistent, small, easily-manageable chunks of time that you will come to love and look forward to.

Most people will be highly motivated for the first few days of attempting personal growth and then slack off and drop the activity. This is pretty common and understandable when you rely only on personal motivation to get the job done. By committing to this challenge, you aren't relying solely on your own willpower - you have a goal and a team to help you get there!

And that is the reason for the 90-day challenge. It is a way to focus on a goal - building a habit that will improve your life - and make it stick. It's a way to organize yourself to get the work done, and there will be work. That's where your team comes in! We're here to help you get started and show you how to finish strong.

You can do this!

Join the Ranks of Amazing Meditators Worldwide

Meditating can make you superhuman! Don't believe me? Check out these names and tell me they aren't above average in some way.

- Wayne Dyer - self-help author and motivational speaker who wrote over 40 books
- Eckhart Tolle - spiritual mindfulness teacher
- Oprah Winfrey - American Media Executive, philanthropist, and also used to have some sort of talk show
- David Lynch - filmmaker and director - "The thing about meditation is that you become more and more you."
- Deepak Chopra - author
- The Beatles - wrote a few songs you may have heard once or twice
- The Beach Boys - also wrote a few songs you may have heard once
- Sting - same thing, wrote and performed some songs

- Katy Perry- famous musical artist – has stated in interviews that meditation "puts me in the best mood."
- Sheryl Crow – used meditation to help with her recovery from cancer
- Russell Simmons - CEO of Def Jam Records and author of Success Through Stillness: Meditation Made Simple
- Ellen DeGeneres - comedian and talk-show host
- Howard Stern - radio personality
- William Clay Ford Jr., Executive Chairman of Ford Motor Company
- Steve Jobs - worked for some company named Apple
- Hugh Jackman - developed the ability to grow razor-sharp metal claws - in the movies, at least!
- Russell Brand - famous comedian
- Jerry Seinfeld - another famous comedian - are you seeing any connection between creativity and meditation yet?

But by far one of the most famous names of all time is Siddhartha Gautama, AKA the Buddha - maybe you've heard of him? His meditation exploits were so revolutionary, he literally affected the lives of millions of humans to follow!

Why do so many highly productive people use meditation? They all report that it helps them deal with stress and change, and it lets them start the day with a little more emotional stability. Success can bring more challenges than a person may be ready to take on. To stay functional at high levels of creativity, a huge number of these unique individuals use meditation. And, in turn, they advocate that everyone around them should be doing it too.

One example is how Oprah Winfrey encourages everyone working for her at Harpo Productions, Inc to take the meditation classes that she organizes for them. She claims that this has helped the entire company to reach their goals, as well as improved their personal relationships away from work, and even helped them sleep better at night.

William Ford used meditation to get through several hard, dark years of bankruptcy, and since then, he has promoted yoga as well as mindfulness classes at the Ford Motor Company. This is to help ensure that his employees are their best and most productive, creative selves.

Katy Perry learned Transcendental Meditation to help deal with the many stresses of living on the road. Her highly successful music career has her traveling non-stop, and meditation is her method of making it tolerable. She found it so helpful, she taught it to her road crew as well.

All these people believe in and use meditation as a daily aid, and there's no doubt that it has had massive effects on their success as artists, authors, public personalities, and religious world influencers. If you are capable of reading and understanding these words, then you have the basic prerequisites to learn how to meditate and gain at least one of the abilities that they all had in common. Could it help you in life as much as it has helped them? We believe the answer is yes.

Not only the rich and famous have stressful lives, of course. Why aren't we using the same tools to keep stress levels down and increase creativity? Here are just a few jobs and positions that could benefit from an increase in the ability to maintain an even mental/ emotional keel:

- Anyone in a leadership position. On top of responsibilities for budgets and deadlines, there are all the issues that come up from managing people.
- Investment professionals. Keeping your cool when dealing with market fluctuations and making decisions on large amounts of capital generates a lot of stress.
- Anyone working with deadlines and project completion dates. Programmers, engineers, sales professionals, etc. may be on a tight schedule to get a specific result or project completed. It can be hard to keep focused and creative when under the gun.
- Customer services representatives. From food serving to reception to call centers, these jobs have so many stressful challenges.
- Teachers – students of all levels and ages present their own challenges to the one

teaching. Working at your highest level in this industry can be hard to maintain without the right tools to keep you centered.

Some Common Questions and Concerns

We would like to touch on a few things right off the bat before we get to all the amazing benefits that you can get from sitting. If you haven't done much meditation, some of these doubts might be holding you back.

What is meditation, anyway? Does that mean to have zero thoughts?

Meditation is the use of a technique to focus your mind on an activity, thought, or object, to train your mind and find a mental or emotional state that is separate from the normal daily mind process. This is not a way to stop your mind, but instead, a way to slow it down and observe what it's doing. As you meditate, you are training your mind, increasing your ability to concentrate, and building the ability to direct your attention. It's doubtful that you will ever have zero thoughts for extended periods while you are still on Earth, and that is definitely not our goal with this challenge.

Don't I have to be religious to meditate?

You don't have to believe in a deity or supernatural entity, or "the force," to meditate. Many meditation teachers are respected scientists, psychologists, or other Western professionals, following a less traditional path. But if you do believe in and have faith in a specific religion, you can still practice meditation.

I'm a Christian. Isn't meditation an Eastern religion thing only?

Many Christian people have used meditation over the years - it features in most major religions. We will discuss this a little more in the next chapter, but rest assured, it doesn't break any rules to sit peacefully and focus on your breath.

Is meditation dangerous?

Meditation could be dangerous if you picked the wrong place to practice it. I'm thinking in the middle of a busy street, while behind the wheel, could be a dangerous place. We aren't aware of any danger following our simple meditation plan. If you think that in your specific situation it is too dangerous to sit quietly and contemplatively, then please pick a less risky activity, like eating junk food or texting while walking.

How do I know whether I'm doing it wrong or not?

This is something that most of us think at some point or another. But as Allan Lokos, author and founder of The Community Meditation Center in New York City, said, "So what is a good meditator? The one who meditates." The trick is to not worry about achieving some sort of goal. You are here to practice meditation. And you practice by showing up and doing it. Avoid criticizing and judging your every move. "I lost track and started thinking about Battlestar Galactica again! D'oh!" Just pick up where you left off and show up again tomorrow. Meditation is hard to do wrong; if you are doing it, you're winning!

What type of meditation should I do? There are so many!

It can seem confusing when you look at all the information out there. But if you stick with our simple breath awareness technique for the moment, you will be performing a method similar to that used in a variety of medical studies worldwide. This maximizes the chances that you will gain the same benefits that all those test subject did.

After you try this simple technique as a starter point, you can look into other options and see if you want to continue down another path. Just like one size fits all clothing, a one size fits all meditation practice is a bad idea. Unless you like baggy jumpers with lots of extra material.

And speaking of health or mental benefits, that's what we want to cover in the next chapter. Prepare to be amazed by all of the effects a daily meditation practice can give you as you complete the 90-day challenge!

Start Now! Day 1

We hope that all the fantastic and positive knowledge from this chapter has given you even more reason to start your meditation practice. There's no time like the present to get going. Find a spot to plant yourself and spend five minutes watching your breath.

We will give more instructions in chapter four, but that's so far away right now. You can skip ahead and read the instructions for day one to ten if you like, or you can just use this brief primer to "get the feet wet."

1. Sit with your back in a neutral position. Don't sit on a soft chair or couch that has you leaning back, either sit cross-legged with a pillow lifting your butt or a stiff-backed chair. Tim uses an office chair in the locked position so it won't recline, or he uses a meditation cushion on top of a yoga mat. Don't worry about the lotus position; we don't use it!
2. Take a few deep breaths and release them, just let the cares of the day slip away for a few minutes. You can start

worrying again in five minutes! Put any devices on "Do Not Disturb" so no one will text you or send you an email and bother you. The world can wait for this brief time.

3. Set a timer on your phone or another device, double check to make sure it's running and set it aside. Tell yourself that you won't check to make sure it's still working or to see how much longer. Your job is to practice for the full 5 minutes.

4. Just watch your breath and feel it go in and out. You don't have to make it do anything. Just let it happen, and watch. Feel your chest rise, then fall. You could say "rise" to yourself on each intake of breath, and then "fall" each time you breathe out.

5. If you lose track and then realize you aren't paying attention to your breaths, don't sweat it. Just start again. That's part of the process. You will go off on a tangent, maybe worrying if you got the instructions right, or remember that you need to pick up Johnny at 2:00, etc. Don't be hard on yourself, just get back to it and

worry about Johnny after you're done here. He'll understand.

6. You might have an itch or something or feel like you need to fix your shirt. Some instructions tell you to suck it up and just sit there itching and all unadjusted. Our instructions in this challenge say to wait as long as you can before moving and observe the sensations, then go ahead and scratch the itch, while paying deliberate attention to the act. Then go back to watching your breath.

7. Keep going until that timer goes off. Stay with it no matter what! The only excuses for quitting early are: a crying baby that you are only the caregiver for, a Roomba that repeatedly slams into you because you forgot to disable it beforehand, or being shot at by spies that are after the secret plans.

Success! You have now started on the 90-day Meditation Challenge! It's all downhill from here!

This Chapter's Key Takeaway Points:

- Anyone who can read this book and understand it is capable of meditating
- Meditation is non-denominational, crossing all faiths and groups
- Scientific evidence proves that lasting habits and change can result from the completion of a new behavior for at least 66 or more days consecutively, so a 90-day challenge is a great way to build a meditation practice that lasts
- Thousands of famous people use meditation daily to help lower stress, keep on top of their busy schedules, and advance their goals
- Kyla is a meditation and yoga teacher who has practical experience living and teaching a meditative lifestyle
- Tim is an author, Heartmath Coach, and construction worker who is afraid of bees and clowns and meditates to keep calm around said bees and clowns

CHAPTER 2

MEDITATION IS GOOD FOR YOU!

There are a lot of reasons that everyone should learn to meditate. We know you have an idea that this is true already, or you wouldn't be here with us right now, but we want to make sure you have a really good feeling about the facts and benefits. This will give you more motivation and staying power for the day that you really aren't feeling it. But first, a quick recap of what came before.

History of Meditation - A Very Brief Recounting

Meditation has been practiced by all major spiritual traditions over the centuries, including

Christianity, Buddhism, and Hinduism. The fact that so many found meditation useful over the centuries points to how much those people must have gotten from it. Otherwise, it wouldn't have been used so much! The point we want to make is that meditation has been a useful tool across many cultures and religions, and it still has plenty to teach modern humanity too.

The earliest known evidence of meditation being practiced is from all the way before 3500 BCE, in India. In ancient times, meditation was for religious folk, not for itinerant construction workers like Tim or for any other commoners. Yogis, ascetic monks, and hermits used abstention and hardship to try to achieve their spiritual goals. The focus was to understand and grow closer to a higher being. What we now practice as yoga comes from this far ago time, but our focus is a lot different! While in modern times, a lot of people go to yoga classes for reasons such as health, flexibility, and coolness factor, originally, it is thought to have been developed to prepare the body and mind for meditation practices.

Buddhism was formed from these earlier practices by Siddhartha Gautama in the 6th century BCE after he achieved enlightenment through his own experiences. Many Western styles of meditation are heavily influenced by his teachings. With Buddhism, the focus has shifted from knowledge of a higher power to understanding your own true nature and ending suffering.

Zen Buddhism is a famous branch of this religion, with heavy influences from Taoism. This meditation practice is now taught in many different countries, although it is reputed to be a "vigorous" and difficult path, which isn't for everyone. It involves sitting "zazen" in the most famous Japanese forms, and the study of koans. Most people interested in meditation have heard of these riddles. For example, "Two hands clap and there is a sound; what is the sound of one hand?" This is a quite famous koan.

The basic Christian meditation is very similar to many others, although it was, of course, developed after AD 36. One form involves sitting with your back straight in a quiet place, breathing normally, and letting your mind still. This might be done by saying a word to yourself, such as the ancient Christian prayer word Maranatha, said with each of the four syllables emphasized. The meditator is instructed to just return to the word if they realize they wandered off in their head and stopped repeating it. The meditation might be done for 20 or 30 minutes, twice a day. Other Christian meditations are done by focusing on or repeating specific scriptures.

Why Do We Want to Meditate?

This 90-day challenge is like a gym membership for your brain!

People have lots of reasons that they think it might be a good idea to be meditating. A lot of people want relief from mental and physical stress. Some people think that meditation will fill in some of the need they have for purpose and meaning in their lives, get them closer to the source. Some have heard of finding nirvana. Other people think it looks cool. Still other people think that they will gain mystical powers and travel the astral plane. Some (or all?) of these things may be possible for you. Another way of approaching this is to think of it as mental training.

We understand why it's so popular to go to the gym and work out, try to eat healthily, and, in general, attempt to do things that will make your body look and feel great. There is a recognizable advantage and a reason for these behaviors: they make you feel good, they make others react favorably to your body, they keep you healthy. Yoga is becoming more and more widespread because it supports a healthy body, among other reasons. It's widely accepted that physical activity and a healthy diet are in your best interest.

We know that our body's "natural" state is one where we eat whatever is put in front of us, we sit around and sleep in, and we never just jump up and run a few miles. That's unnatural, running for no reason! Our default position for the body is, in general, a little lumpy, not very flexible, and an unhealthy color from too much time indoors. To become the "real" you, you need to do things like eat broccoli and salad once in a while instead of grilled cheese sandwiches and fries. You need to get your heart rate up and move something heavy around, stretch out your tendons and get the lymph fluid moving. Your body has inertia, and you need to defeat that to get in shape. Very few people will do this "naturally."

The brain is no different. It has a default state too. Garbage in, garbage out - your mind is preloaded with information from your surroundings, such as your childhood, your workplace, Netflix, and what happened in Vegas last year. Your brain's natural state is a little lumpy, not very flexible, and an unhealthy shade of gray from too much time staring at a tiny little screen.

When we see a scrawny person walk up to a really heavy weight, say 100 pounds, we know they will have a hard time lifting it. Everyone accepts that to get the ability to do things like lift heavy things or ski down really steep hills without dying or run a marathon, we need to spend time and effort training the body. So why don't we think about training the mind?

When we see a mentally scrawny person approach a difficult situation, like a loss in the family, we, of course, can't see that their brain hasn't been to the gym. We expect our undeveloped brains to be able to do the heavy lifting in life, with no training and no preparation. So when this unprepared and devastated person has a mental breakdown from grief or depression, it should be no surprise, but it might have been mitigated.

We suffer from addictions, depression, fear, anger, mood swings, and many other conditions that have a huge mental or emotional component as well as, in some cases, physical causes. Why do we expect our untrained, unworked out, scrawny brain to be able to lift all this weight? Probably because we never thought about it or had this idea presented to us.

What if there was a way to get a workout for your mind that would: increase your inner calmness and flexibility, reduce your stress levels, lower your reactivity, increase your happiness, and cost nearly nothing? You already know where I'm going with this. Meditation is one way to work out the brain. Our prediction is that, someday soon, it will be as common to meditate as it is to see people using a treadmill or pumping iron. And that is when the human race will really start to advance, when we start thinking that mental and emotional health is as important as a well-muscled, slim body. When we become as concerned about our mental exercises and our intake of uplifting reading material as we are about High Intensity Interval Training and protein shakes, we will finally be able to look past the way the body looks, to its overall function, including mental and spiritual.

Health Benefits

Let's look at meditation from a strictly physical point of view and see what change in the body can result from sitting still and being mindful. Meditation has been a subject of study for decades now, and there's a lot of good information out there that verifies what it can do for a body.

You've probably heard that meditation can reduce or lower stress. But how does it do that? To get the answer, we have to get a brief overview of what exactly is going on in your body when you "feel stressed" by the various life events around you.

Let's imagine a stressful situation, such as being late for an important meeting or being cut off in traffic by some nutcase driving a Toyota or being chased by a pack of clowns. You have a highly useful, instinctive reaction to events like this. Your body uses hormones such as cortisol to get you ready to take on predators, run, etc. This is the much talked about fight or flight reflex, and it is a necessary part of living in this world. Or, at least, it used to be a necessary thing. In our day-to-day lives, it's less likely in this century to need a huge burst of adrenaline to help us run away from those clowns.

The problems for your body and mind result from elevated levels of stress hormones, which never go down. You don't need to be in fight or flight for days, weeks, or months on end, but this is what happens for almost every human being in the modern era. We get excited by an external event or condition, and then deal with the issue at that time. Then, the background stress residue hangs out in the body causing mayhem. There isn't a signal to return to the pre-stress situation. This ends up changing the hormone balance and functioning of many systems and can help cause issues such as high blood pressure and inflammation. Inflammation of body tissues is a contributor to many diseases and conditions that we don't want to experience, like arthritis. Other effects of elevated cortisol levels include weight gain, higher cholesterol levels, decreased bone density, and heart disease.

And now the good news. Meditation seems to be very effective at reducing cortisol levels in the bloodstream by up to fifty percent, back to a healthier level. Multiple studies around the world have results that suggest meditation and mindfulness are the answer to chronic high levels of stress. One, published by Dr. Elizabeth Hoge, an associate professor at Georgetown University Medical Center's Department of Psychiatry, found that stress hormones could be reduced by up to 15% with an 8-week daily practice.

One reason that meditation gets these results could be how it affects the vagus nerve. The vagus nerve runs from the brainstem to the abdomen, connecting a lot of our systems together. It is tied in to our circulatory system and heart rate, our digestion, our breathing, and many others. The vagus nerve is a part of the autonomic nervous system, which runs most of our bodies without our help. But since it is a mostly unconscious system, when we get stressed, we can't do much about it by just deciding to.

When we meditate, this stimulates the vagus nerve and helps us to get out of fight or flight mode. So when we sit quietly, follow our breaths, and notice our thoughts, we are affecting the vagus nerve, along with every single system it's connected to.

Another physical effect on the body is that parts of the brain can actually grow in size as well as density. A study done in Massachusetts General Hospital by Harvard researchers used MRI scanning on the participants before and after an 8-week meditation program. They used a weekly meeting as well as daily practice of over 20 minutes on their own. The results were that the hippocampus increased in density. This area is linked with spatial memory, navigation, and memory storage.

At the same time, the participants were found to have a reduction of density in the amygdala. This part of the brain has been linked with negative emotions. Fear and the events that trigger fear are processed in part through the right hemisphere of the amygdala. Lowered levels of stress could be because of this effect that meditating regularly has on the brain.

Meditation affects the prefrontal cortex too. This area has been shown to affect things like binge eating and addictions to alcohol and cigarettes. Increased density in this part can help with addictive behavior, letting you get control over any problems with those issues.

You may have heard that stress can age a person, and it's true. One way that this happens is by the shortening of your telomeres. A telomere is an end cap on a DNA strand, a lot like the cap on a shoelace that stops a lace from unraveling. As we age, and our cells divide, these telomeres get a little bit shorter each time. We have an enzyme called telomerase that has the job of repairing and maintaining the telomeres. When stress hormones and inflammation interrupt the healthy functioning of the body, we don't produce enough telomerase. This increases the aging rate as the wear and tear on our cells goes up.

Meditation has been found to increase telomerase activity in the immune cells for those with a daily practice of sitting. This could be why seasoned meditators are reported to look years younger than their chronological age.

Another effect of meditation and mindfulness practices is the increase of glutathione or GSH. This is a powerful antioxidant that the cells need to remove free radicals, which are known to damage DNA and, thereby, cause aging at an increased rate. GSH also assists in protecting us from environmental toxins and boosts the immune system. This is one more reason that meditation can slow aging, by helping our bodies to produce glutathione.

So, let's recap some of the physical benefits of meditation when it is used regularly. And don't just take our word for it. Do some research if you like, and you will find a lot of information out there that backs all of this up.

- Meditation reduces stress hormones and allows recovery from stress
- It decreases inflammation in the body
- It reduces heart attack and stroke risk
- Cholesterol levels can drop
- Reduces free radicals floating around destroying your body
- Reduces allergies and improves skin condition
- Reduces chronic pain from things like arthritis
- Lowers blood sugar levels
- Helps with weight loss

And a whole lot more! I'm sure you can see that your body needs this in its daily routine.

Effects of Meditation on the Mind

From our arrival on this planet, we are programmed by the experiences we encounter. Our families, schools, friends. These experiences shape our mind, determine our views and reactions to life. The coping mechanisms that we put in place or have been taught become our patterns. The human mind loves patterns, and we create them wherever we can as they offer a great sense of security. Meditation gives us the opportunity to look at our programming and the patterns that support it, allowing us to change our reactions and define a life we want to live. Be the person we want to be. The patterns of the mind were, at one point in time, implemented to keep you safe. The subconscious has come to rely on these beliefs and patterns as a sense of security, like a warm blanket or a wall between us and possible harm.

It does not know who it is beyond the programs, so it does not want to surrender them willingly. The untrained mind is either in the past or the future, often disconnecting us from what exists here in the present moment. Consumed with our tightly scheduled lives, perhaps relationship disagreements or financial worries consume us. We have this dialog that takes place, and it can range from outward judgment of others or inward judgment of ourselves.

For example, imagine you are driving to work with only minutes to spare, and the traffic slows. Maybe you become impatient with others, as, in your racing mind, the slightest upset becomes an issue of serious emotional reaction. It takes a little old lady a little too long to cross the road. In an uncluttered mind, compassion would be easy to find for the old lady, understanding that age slows us, and she didn't purposely set out to make you late for your meeting. In a cluttered mind, the ticking seconds would become unbearable. "COME ON LADY!" Or, a person can start a series of self-blaming thoughts. "You idiot! Why didn't you leave five minutes early!" or "You're so stupid." Outward or inward, these thoughts create a tense physical response in the body. Anger engages, and we release hormones to support this emotional reaction. Pupils dilate, the heart races, and the muscles tense. In the case of sadness or guilt, our hormones are blocked and organs slow. Both useful responses when needed, both very important for survival. Difficulties can arise in both mind and body if we are constantly riding these emotions, and the mind cannot rest in a neutral space.

Anger allows us to create a change in our environment, to either get away from the situation or engage in self-defense. But when there's no need to take violent and angry action, either physically or with our words, all that results is a buildup of toxic hormones. This leads to stress that never needed to exist. Sadness or disappointment allows us to try to change the outcome next time. It gives room for growth and can deepen self-awareness. Issues arise when we are continuously riding the emotional state of the mind, and our physical bodies are responding. Meditation seeks a neutral mind, a mind that isn't continuously judging good and bad, danger no danger. It is simply watching life as it is.

Continuous practice of meditation allows us the opportunity to observe our thoughts and physicality, while simultaneously cultivating a deep sense of self-awareness. We switch from repressing our thoughts or allowing to them to run wild (both these options lead to unfavorable emotional responses), to observing and contemplating the validity and the value of the thoughts as they arise. If we repress our thoughts and emotions, eventually, they bottle up, potentially causing physical illness or large emotional outbursts. Or if the mind is left to run wild, this often leads to bouts of anxiety and depression. These mental states cause mental stress and directly influence the physical body. It is important to remember when working with the mind, it's like training a puppy: it is important to NOT beat the puppy into submission. Self-understanding and compassion are the quickest way to a silent mind. Use humor instead of criticism, learn to giggle at yourself and the ridiculousness of your thoughts. **Meditation truly is the art of not taking ourselves so seriously**. Invite a sense of play to your practice as well as your life. Understanding that inner peace is cultivated in every single breath we take. The possibilities are limitless in its use.

Meditation will allow the practitioner to observe the thoughts that their mind is having. We learn, over time, to observe the thoughts as though you are watching a movie. As you build your skills, it becomes more and more apparent of thoughts that serve your highest good and those that do not. This is the space where you can start to choose how you react, and how you will live your life without beating the puppy that is your mind. You can take that puppy to obedience training by meditating and teach him to stop chewing all the shoes!

Meditation and Mindfulness Can Dilate Time

An unanticipated side effect of mindfulness that hardly anyone mentions, is the effect it has on the flow of time. This is an issue of the perception of how time flows more than anything. Here is how meditation and mindfulness have affected Tim's time flow:

"Before I started meditating regularly, everything was blurring together so that the years started flying by like a steadily flapping crow of doom that has a really important destination and has no time for sitting still. At the rate it was moving, I was getting worried that old age was nearly upon me, in my early 40s!

Then I started sitting and observing myself, my breathing and thoughts. Over weeks, time slowed down and even started crawling. What happened here, did I actually slow down time?

I like to think I did! It's one of those Jedi mind tricks, right?

But really, what happened was that I started paying attention to life for the first time, instead of living in the past and the future so much. And as I paid attention to my interactions with the world, I started making deeper, richer memories. I added details to my knowledge of things around me.

An example would be an hour-long drive from one place in our huge province to the next. Instead of zoning out and listening to the radio like a zombie, I started noticing that I was driving past forest, rivers, and other drivers!

Instead of only thinking about what I was going to do when I got there, I just started existing in the car, actually being in my body. Instead of going over what I should have said in an endless thought-loop or worrying about how to talk to so and so when I next saw him, I noticed a flock of water birds in a pond and came out of zombie mode. And time slowly started stretching out.

With time running longer, I thought this would be a problem when I was "trapped" at work or in a lineup. And granted, these still aren't my favorite things. So now that I'm stuck at work for hours on end, it really does seem like a longer period. The weird thing is, I don't mind that much. Because even though it might seem like each day lasts forever, this is a bonus when I'm not at work or stuck driving.

Now, when I have a day off, I pay attention to that too. For me, mindfulness means that a two-week vacation lasts for what seems like months. A lazy Sunday stretches on forever. In this sense, I am totally winning the game of life. I'm looking forward to the second half of my life since I'm in the middle area. It took a short 50 years to get to here. The second half is going to seem like it's about a hundred years or more! I plan on being present for every single moment from here on in.

Yeah, this means that the unpleasant experiences last a while too. The key is in the lack of judgment. Somehow, I just do the things and let the experience exist. I still try to fix my situation if there's a way to make it better, but I endure and pay attention through the downer times."

Key Takeaway Points From chapter 2

- **Meditation causes measurable changes in the body and brain**
- **It lowers cortisol levels, which reduces inflammation while lowering stress levels**
- **Meditation has many effects that can help you live a longer and healthier life**
- **Mindfulness meditation can cause changes in the structure of the brain which assist in lowering stress and coping with addictive patterns of behavior**

- Telomeres have been shown to stop shortening, or even lengthen, as a person becomes a proficient meditator so that, over time, a meditator can increase their lifespan
- Destructive patterns of behavior can slowly be interrupted or altered by meditation, allowing a person to change their outcomes
- Meditation and mindfulness can help you slow down and appreciate life, so that time seems to slow down. Who wants to rush to their grave full tilt without stopping to smell the roses?

CHAPTER 3

HOW THE HECK DO WE DO THIS MEDITATION THING?

The Basics

I'm sure if you're still with us, you're impressed by all the amazing things that meditation is going to do for you. Who wouldn't want all those effects to start taking place in your body, mind, and soul? No one would turn all that down!

And you've already started your first day of the challenge, right? I know that you went ahead and started Day 1, just like we asked, and you will have no trouble continuing with this 90-day challenge. (If you didn't start, then what are you waiting for? Get on it!)

So before we get into the structure of the rest of the challenge, let's look at some basic ways to make it more effective and easier to accomplish the daily practice.

The very first thing we want to do is to make it convenient, accessible, and easy to get to the pillow or chair. The more convenient and easier it is, the less willpower will be required to do it. If there was a way to set it up so that you would get up in the morning and stumble into the meditation tractor beam, which would pull you in and slap your butt on that pillow, then that's what we would want to set up for ourselves. Beam me onto the mat, Scotty!

Sadly, there are no tractor beams as yet. While we wait for science fact to catch up with science fiction, we will just have to do our best to line things up ahead of time. We want you to plan a little and do some prep work. If you know, for instance, that you will be meditating in your home office first thing in the morning, then set an alarm to notify you what time to start. This will hopefully pull you away from Facebook if you get distracted when you get up.

Next, the night before, make sure any props or items that you will be using are already set up. If you are going to be sitting in a chair, have it in the spot you will be using it. If it's a meditation pillow, put it where you will need it. If you have a special timer that you use, put it on the pillow. Make everything dead simple so that even a braindead morning zombie could figure it out.

And speaking of braindead morning zombies, getting enough sleep is also important. If you are really sleep deprived, then you might have a hard time sitting and concentrating without dozing off. Try to get as much rest as you will need to be able to focus on meditation. This will help you in all areas of your life; you will be healthier, better able to focus at work, and less likely to wrap your car around a telephone pole when you pass out while driving. The side benefit will be an easier time staying awake for meditation!

Setting For Sitting: The Sitting Setting

> *"Be here now. Be someplace else later. Is that so complicated?"*
> -David M. Bader

Where will you be meditating for this challenge? You might be lucky and have a spare bedroom that you can use whenever you want, or a home office, a garage, or basement. If this is you, then you can dedicate that space to your practice and leave items there to be ready for each use. But maybe your living situation is full of complicated distractions that will interrupt you. More thought might be needed to get you set up for success. If you travel a lot, for instance, you will need to decide what items you must have for meditation and find a way to always pack those. A bulky pillow will most likely be out of the question.

It would be helpful to find a place that is reasonably quiet, and not too cold/ warm/ breezy. If possible, no one should be playing with a PlayStation on a large screen in your vicinity while you sit. There shouldn't be any machinery that will kick on and kick you out of your zone, like a washing machine going from one cycle to another. It would be preferable if you can avoid trying to meditate where a door could open and slam shut at any moment, too.

The one environmental factor that will definitely be too much to handle is body contact while your eyes are closed. You have to be where no person or animal will touch you or rub up against you. Having a 3-year-old daughter jump on your lap or Fido licking your face is not going to help the process. This will mean you will have to adjust the timing so these distractors aren't there or go to a place where they can't reach you.

If you live with unsupportive roommates or family members, you won't want them bothering you, or maybe even aware of what you're doing. In these cases, you might have to meditate somewhere else. Some people choose their car before they go into work, or a park bench, or even a stairwell that few use. Think about alternative spots that will let you sit without your unsupportive or negative human influences. Also, don't let them know you are doing this challenge. They might take the wind out of your sails with their comments and remarks.

If you have to, go to the bathroom and lock the door. This is one location that you should be able to get five minutes to yourself. This location comes with a built-in meditation throne, but you could also put a cushion on the floor.

Meditation Altar or Shrines

If you have a space to yourself, and you are interested in making yourself a meditation altar, this can be an excellent way to get in the proper frame of mind for meditating. This could be a corner of a desk or a small table, or a placemat that you put out with some special items on it, or something more elaborate. Altars have been made inside closets, on patios and decks, even in gardens. Creating your own sacred space is an awesome idea, and well worth it if it helps you keep up your meditation practice. Searching on

Pinterest for meditation altars gives lots of ideas for your special space.

Once you have chosen where you will build your altar, gather items that feel sacred or special to you. It's important to only include objects that match the intention you have for the space. Good choices are gemstones and crystals, religious figurines, pictures of mountains or trees, incense, a candle, or a singing bowl. Tim's collection of magnetic hematite stones and coins from Mexico are his portable shrine that he takes with him when away from home.

So once you've gone to the trouble of creating this special place, your refuge, you will have to make sure you keep it clean. This is going to require some dusting, and you need to make sure that a big stack of bills or a bunch of half-full glasses of water don't accumulate here. All these contaminated objects will have to be kept somewhere else.

Your little shrine can become a soothing part of your daily ritual, as you sit in front of or near it and begin your practice. It will be a signal to your mind that it's time to pay attention and be a good addition to the habit formation we are trying for.

One thing to bear in mind, don't put off meditating until you have the altar! Start now! Getting everything "just right" before you can start is a great excuse you could use to put off ever starting... It can be a work in progress while you continue with the challenge. This would give you a chance to put some thought into the items you will need and gather them up.

Distractions

> "If you can't meditate in a boiler room, you can't meditate."
> -Alan Watts

Many people have the idea that meditation can only take place in a perfect, silent location with a comfortable temperature, soft padding, low lighting, etc. If this were the case, most people would never be able to practice it. These kinds of places are really hard to find!

You just won't be able to eliminate all distractions unless you build a soundproof room. And even then, you will take yourself inside, and the beating of your heart will eventually be a huge distraction, or you might be able to hear a gentle wheeze coming from your left nostril because you're a little stuffed up. Some noises will be unavoidable, so instead, incorporate them into your routine.

You can learn to become aware of the noise, and also aware of your reaction to it. It can be a great opportunity to see your mind in action, watching it think angry thoughts about the neighbor's dog, producing the sense of annoyance at the street noises and car horns. And through it all, suddenly remembering to be in the moment.

So, do your best to find a peaceful spot to practice sitting in, free from distractions. And if you can't find the "perfect" environment, meditate anyway!

It will be better to start and risk getting thrown off your game when some noise might jar you out of your rhythm than to not get into your practice at all. Learning to meditate with a low level of noises and distractions can be very freeing. This is how Tim became able to sit in an airport waiting for a plane at 5:00 AM and still fit in his daily practice. He was already used to people walking around and doing annoying things because he was meditating in the living room at home with multiple annoying distractions for weeks before that day! And no, he is not suggesting that his wife is annoying, so when she reads this, she will hopefully remember how much he loves her.

Maybe dealing with noise isn't something you really want to worry about right now. It can be a lot to try to cope with, especially something like the crying baby next door or a jackhammer right under your window. If you know that you won't be able to deal with the noises, earplugs are one option, and noise-canceling headphones with a light meditation track playing are another. Starting out with these kinds of aids is a real benefit for some. Go ahead and use whatever you need to, and don't feel like you're cheating. I mean, you are, but it's all good. If ancient monks had noise-canceling headphones and

MP3s, maybe they would have been using them too.

Suppose you are going to try meditation on the subway or at a bench in the park. In a case like this, wearing earbuds or Airpods means that no one should be coming over trying to talk to you and disturbing your meditation, and maybe let you slip under the radar. No one needs to know that you are in your special zone, you just look like a music lover. This is something Tim does often. There doesn't actually have to be any music playing for this to be effective, and with modern wireless Bluetooth headphones, no one would even know if they weren't turned on. In general, people aren't mindful of their surroundings in any case. They will see the headset, assume you are listening to Bohemian Rhapsody by Queen, and go away.

Noise isn't going to be the only distraction, of course. There will be pains in the body, itches, and all manner of other things that are going to try to get you to focus on them instead of what you sat down to focus on. This is kind of the point; to learn to notice these things and still maintain focus on your chosen goal. So it really is counterproductive to try to eliminate every distraction. If you somehow succeed, you will just create more out of your own thought stuff.

Kyla's Viewpoint on Distractions:

"As you learn to arrive in meditative space, please remember that it takes time. Even though we appear to be doing nothing, it's in doing nothing that something happens. Being gentle with yourself in the process is of the utmost importance. We are not seeking non-thought, but the experience of the moment. Accepting what comes as it is. Life is continuously happening around us, and it's really what we are trying to accept, this truly is the trick. Accepting the little noises; if the neighbor's dog is barking, he is just being a dog, and that's how dogs communicate. The tightness you may feel in your shoulders or neck is life's weight resting on them. What, in this very moment, can we do about it? I would suggest applying the breath, focusing your mind on breathing into the tension and releasing it with the exhalation. Let it go. Notice the sensations that surround you and are within you, and do not let the mind engage in judgmental thought. Just see it as it is. After your sitting session, you can apply the knowledge you have gathered. If your shoulder was tight, it's just your body's way of suggesting a stretch or two. If your mind was attached to a disagreeable situation with another person, perhaps an evaluation of how we let others affect us. Why are you letting this disagreeable person take your self-care time, didn't the situation at the time it happened take enough of your time? It really is our choice.

Meditation gives us space to choose how we spend our time. With the practice of observation, it becomes clearer and clearer on where we are expending our mental energies. It has been said that the mind itself is not capable of original thought, that it either repeats past experiences or wanders into the futures of various outcomes. The problem with either of these mental states is that we cannot change the past. Sometimes the mind replays a place of happier times, or it clings to a past tragedy in the hope of not repeating it. Either way, it rests as it is, and all we can do is either find gratitude for those beautiful moments or accept that the trauma of a terrible situation has ended. Fear of it happening again is blocking us from a potentially beautiful experience. It is here, in the moment, this one single breath of connection, where we are free. I have often suggested to my clients to try and find five things to focus on that are right now, in this moment. The sound of the music you have chosen, the rhythm of the breath, the clothes resting against your skin and the soft sensation of the material as your body rises and falls. We have used candles and watched the flames move gently in the atmosphere. If we were practicing outside, even to watch a blade of grass dance in the wind. Just watching it move gently. I am a huge advocate for breath, and my advice is always to start there. It is always with you, and if not… You are no longer with us. It is reliable and constant, and you need nothing beyond it. It is the simplest form of pleasure if you allow it. Simply repeating to yourself. Breathe in… and feel the inhalation, and then Breathe out and stay with the exhalation works beautifully. Please remember that any moment spent in connection with the breath is a moment spent in meditation. We collect these moments like raindrops in a bucket. Just like it takes time for a tree to produce its fruit, as does the mind in creating peace. We are only seeking to master this moment. This one single breath. So let the pressure go and enjoy. Let yourself feel just this one breath and then let it rise into another. It was told to me once that the moment rests in the space between the inhalation and the exhalation. The small break that takes place between the rise and fall of the breath; see if you can find it. Again, and again."

Timing

To a degree, when you meditate is up to personal preference. But there are several strong arguments that getting your practice in first thing in the morning and then at the end of the day are the most beneficial times. Let's talk about the morning first.

Having a positive morning ritual is the best way to get yourself out the door on the right foot. Starting out with a calm, positive mind has the potential to send a ripple through your entire life. It could help you in so many ways, such as better communication with kids/ spouse/ roommates for starters. Mindfulness could lead to better breakfast and dietary habits, which could make you healthier over time. A calm mindset could help in traffic, heading off road rage and a day-long bad mood caused by the terrible driving of others. Having a smile on your face when you get to work because you still feel the peace of your meditation practice could lead to better work performance and less stress. And all of these potential benefits to starting the day off right could mean that you come home at the end of the day still able to be nice to your significant other, so you don't get snappy when you talk about his or her day, and they feel loved. And this means they don't go out late at night to buy piles of McDonald's food and gorge themselves, resulting in heart disease and fear of clowns. And their fear of clowns will distract them from their life purpose, which will cause no end of troubles for everyone.

I'm betting that you now realize that you can make sure your loved ones don't get heart disease or fail to fulfill their life's purpose. If you would only start the day out right and meditate before you leave the house, everything would fall in line. The fate of the world is in your hands.

Meditating near the end of the day could have good effects on your mind right before you go to bed. With reduced stress levels and a calm mind, it will be easier to fall asleep as well as stay sleeping. The events of the day can be unpacked in your mind, and endless ruminating about the recent past might slow down, giving you some mental room to breathe. For these reasons, it is ideal to sit for your second meditation before bedtime. We realize this is a busy time of the day, what with so much to catch up watching on Netflix, but you know that the next episode of Riverdale will still be there tomorrow.

If you're going to work on meditating at the end of the day, the best thing to do is set an alarm on your phone to tell you it's time to go sit. Then you can tell yourself, "That's it! Time to get ready for bed!" and put down your phone/ remote/ tablet, or game controller (or stop folding laundry and cleaning the house, for those of you with a backlog of household chores.

This your 'me' time, dirty laundry will have to wait!).

It is challenging to make a change like this; you can't really see the benefits outweighing the bonus of one last round of video game mayhem or endless Instagram and Facebook scrolling. Consider just trying it, for a day or two, and assessing your results. Tell the others in your life that you will need some space at night for yourself and meditate. Then, without picking up a device and filling your mind with unrest, try going to bed. Some reading of an actual physical book might be acceptable, just no screen time.

The next morning, rate your sleep experience. Did you notice anything different than usual? Did you fall asleep and or stay asleep better or worse than usual? Do you feel rested? What is your overall impression of the experiment?

From Tim's point of view:

"I notice a big difference when I meditate before bed. First off, after sitting for 20 minutes, I just seem to slow down and be in a calm, relaxed state. This makes it easy to go straight to sleep when I lie down if I want. I can read for a while without this state changing much, as long as it's an actual paper book! I wear a Fitbit to track my sleep. What I notice when I meditate before bed is that the Fitbit reports about 15 to 20 minutes more of deep sleep in the early part of the night as opposed to days when I don't meditate. And when I wake up, I seem a bit more alert than normal."

We're sure you now realize that we are in favor of meditating in the morning and then near the end of the day. Maybe these times just aren't practical, so then you must pick another part of the day that matches up with your life.

What would be best is if you could get in a routine of sitting at the same hour every day. This will help make a good habit, as well as ensuring that you remember to sit. It doesn't have to be the moment you spring out of bed. It could be after your first cup of coffee or after your morning shower, or right after another housemate leaves for the day, or after you feed the cat.

But if that just doesn't work for you, then try for right after you get home from work or right before others in the house get home. If you have children that go to bed an hour before you, then after you are sure they are down for the count would be a good time.

Lunchtime or coffee break can be a prime opportunity to sit for a few minutes, practicing your breathing. It might defuse any stress that's been building during the day, dealing with the various issues we all have at our occupations. For those who try meditating on a work break, many report that it gives them a mental second wind and is more effective than coffee for an energizer.

Even if you go with lunchtime, or after returning home, and don't get the maximum benefits that end of day practice would give you, you will still get a lot out of putting your practice anywhere you have to in the day. We want to stress that it's more important to fit a session in somewhere than to not be able to meditate at all because you aren't able to find the "perfect" time. Better late than never. Also, a bird in the hand is worth more than two dead Angry Birds that totally missed knocking down that pig's house when your finger slipped, and they launched incorrectly from the tiny slingshot on your phone screen. Annoying! So, try for morning and night, but if it can't happen, then pick the next best times.

Getting Your Body Ready For Meditation

It's common knowledge that meditation is all about the mind - or is it? We saw in the section on the effect of meditation on the body that there is a strong connection between body and mind. This connection goes both ways. With the proper preparation of the body, sitting on the mat and meditating is much easier. This is how yoga and meditation are connected, and we will explore that in the upcoming chapter The Body and Meditation.

Mental Prep

It can be helpful to be clear on why we are going to all this trouble to meditate. We will be more naturally inclined to accomplish what we set out to do when we know that it is meeting our needs and values. So let's think about what we are most interested in gaining from this activity. If you really want to cement it in there, write it down in a journal.

Some reasons that you could write down to show your personal reason for practicing meditation could be reduced stress, emotional stability, or increased creativity. Here are some sample personal "mission statements" for our 90-day challenge.

- Meditation will help me keep an emotional even keel, to get me through tough days at work
- Meditation will help me de-stress after the day is over so I can sleep easier
- Meditation will make me a better listener and less emotionally reactive with my spouse
- Having meditation as a daily practice will let me be a more understanding and loving parent to my children

- Meditation will allow me to become more mindful and be more present in my own life
- Meditation will give me Jedi mind powers, so I can open doors on the way into the supermarket with a wave of my hand and convince droid hunters to look elsewhere!

We know this might seem like a total waste of time, but making the effort to vocalize or write down your goals and intentions has deep subconscious reverberations. Our intentions do shape our reality, even if we only mean that they give us the motivation to complete a task! Having positive intentions for what you will eventually get from the practice of meditation will keep you working at it, day by day. Always remember that it will take some time to achieve these results. Some things will take much longer; the Jedi mind tricks take the longest! 50 years might be required to get the full effects of telekinesis and droid hunter deflection.

Positive Reinforcement To Build Commitment

> *"When you realize how perfect everything is, you will tilt your head back and laugh at the sky."*
> -Buddha

How can we learn to look forward to our meditation and be more likely to get on that cushion? This is something that seems overlooked in many cases. Part of the problem can be in approaching meditation like a chore, something you have to do, something you really need to use willpower to force yourself into.

Maybe you've heard of those weird people who like washing dishes because it relaxes them. If someone can learn to love dishwashing, then you can enjoy meditation for sure! What we need to do is decode how these weirdos taught themselves to like putting their hands in disgusting dishwater, risking death by impalement on steak knives while simultaneously overcoming their revulsion of greasy food remnants. Because for most of us, we would need to put effort into enjoying this task. Most likely, what they did was pay attention to the positive feelings they were having. They noticed how they were making order out of chaos, cleanliness out of mayhem. They probably admired the soap suds and felt gratitude for warm water. They might feel that they are performing a service for others with their efforts. In other words, they might be using a form of mindfulness, whether on purpose or by accident.

To learn to enjoy your practice, all you need to do is focus on the right aspects of it. As you sit, notice any feelings of comfort in relaxing in the stillness. Feel how nice it is to gently breathe in and out. Be aware of things like the warmth of your sweater, should you be wearing one. Can you sense the tension melting out of your body as your arms gently pull down on your shoulders, lightly tugged by gravity?

Bask in the feeling of having made it onto your cushion, actually sitting and doing the thing! You made it, you are putting yourself first. Be glad. Feel gravity pulling you down, use your mind to "look" at how the mass of your body is anchored to the Earth.

The more pleasant aspects you focus on, the more pleasant aspects you will find. Say "Yes!" to meditation, and you will notice all kinds of little pleasurable sensations. You will become more mindful of the subtle, happy feelings your body is having while it settles into a peaceful rhythm. Enjoy knowing that you are training your mind. Be happy that you can feel the stress leaving you. At times, you might feel the air moving across your skin and give you a delicious little shiver that you can just sit and enjoy as long as it stays with you.

As you build an enjoyment of meditation, you will have an easy time making sure you fit it in. If you miss a session, you will really feel like something was missed!

Another way to positively reinforce the meditation habit is to reward yourself with something you enjoy after each session or after every 10 days, or even after 90 days. It could be something as simple as giving yourself a nice cup of hot chai tea when you're done, for example. Or, on completion of the first 10 days, reward yourself with a trip to the bookstore/ clothing store/ noodle bar, and pick yourself up something nice. How about a big reward for completing the 90-day challenge, like a weekend getaway? The reward has to be something that means something to you, but it doesn't have to mean spending any money. As a reward, you could go for a museum tour if that's your thing.

If you decide to place a reward in the future, make sure you record this on paper, and only let yourself have the reward if you follow through! If you give up on day three, don't reward yourself for being a quitter by picking up a new pair of jeans!

What To Do If You Miss A Day (Or Two)

Things happen to wreck our best-laid plans. You sleep in or you plain forget to meditate, or you stay overnight in a strange location and don't have your special meditation cushion. Or you really want to go see the new Avengers movie, and you will get home too late to sit for the evening. Or you meet up with college buddies and drink more alcohol than any human being ever should. All these things can and will happen, so it's best to accept interruptions in the schedule as a given.

Yes, it would be the best for the challenge if you executed it perfectly, right on schedule. But it isn't necessary to hold yourself to a goal that can be a little unrealistic. You will get all the benefits and make a lifestyle change even if you miss a few practice sessions, so don't sweat it.

What would be important is to make sure you don't miss more than one or at most two sessions in a row. What can happen if you miss three? **It's increasingly likely that for each session you miss, you will drop the whole thing**. The lazy part of our minds, the rotten procrastinator, will jump in there and say things like, "Well, you missed a whole two days. There's no point, it's all a waste of time. You're going to have to start over from the beginning! Might as well wait till next week." And next week might never come. Don't let this happen to you. If you see that it is already happening,

immediately go and find somewhere to meditate. Then you will be back in the game.

What Tim likes to do at a time like this, is to imagine that rotten procrastinator in his head as a person, and then grab that loser by the scruff of his neck and escort him over to a door, throwing him out. "You're not the boss of me!" he imagines yelling. Then he slams the door, puts the Doritos down, and goes to do the thing.

If you miss a day or two, just resolve to get right back at it. If you want, tack those days on the end of the challenge and make it a 92-day challenge. Or don't. This journey is completely in your control. You might remember from the study we talked about in the very beginning of the book that missing one or two sessions had absolutely no effect on forming a habit long term as long as, in general, most of the sessions were completed. The important thing is to make it to the end, not to try to be perfect and feeling guilty if you miss the mark. Perfectionism is not the point of this exercise!

Just can't seem to get it back together after missing a session? Resolve to sit and meditate for just one minute. If you can get yourself to complete a single minute, then consider sitting for a couple more, since you're already there. It would be a shame to waste such a good start, right?

Want to Build a Daily Practice? Don't Let Yourself Make Excuses

Tim's thoughts on excuses and bull$hitting yourself out of making a change or doing a thing:

"When I finally started meditating every day, one thing that changed was that I realized what some of my excuses were for not meditating. I bet a lot of these are common to everyone, at least at first. I decided to eliminate them and just do it!

The first big excuse I previously used to get out of meditation was not having a quiet place of my own to sit. This is a huge hurdle if you let it be one. But there's almost always a way around it, depending on your exact situation. I will admit, it would have been a lot harder if I still had little ones around.

To defeat this excuse, I decided that it just didn't matter. I would sit anywhere I had to, period. I would learn to deal with minor noises, even welcome them as a challenge to my ability to sit through them. I wouldn't worry about earphones or earplugs. I would just be aware of the noise, of my reaction to it, and sit through it.

The next one was being too tired and not able to focus. Again, I determined that this couldn't stop me. Worst case scenario, I would pass out and fall over. A weird thing happened after I thought this through; I never got sleepy while practicing anymore! It was like my subconscious mind knew that trick wouldn't work any longer to get to me to quit.

Here's a tough one: embarrassment. I was embarrassed if anyone saw me meditating, even my wife or children. Almost ashamed, like I was claiming I was better than others. This one I couldn't let stand. I committed to meditating every day, even if it meant sitting in the middle of the living room where someone would walk in. Once I started thinking about it in those terms, I got a lot braver. I decided that I had as much right to meditate wherever I wanted as other people did to stare at their phone screens. After a few days, it didn't bother me as much to know that others were around. I was free to focus on my breathing, even though I was aware of my feeling of insecurity. The next step was purposefully putting myself into situations to try to reduce the feeling through exposure. I ended up sitting on a bench meditating at the mall, sitting in an airport waiting for a flight, and in my truck before work."

Habit Creation Lock-In Master Tricks That You Really Need To Use!

Here are a few ways that we can really lock in a new habit and make sure we follow through. We already have a goal of learning to meditate, but a goal by itself won't do the job. Nearly everyone has the goal of becoming a millionaire, for example, but few make it, and this is because they don't have a system to get them there. We want to make a foolproof system to get you through this challenge. This will have the added benefit of taking you right past the end of the 90 days. If your goal is just to make it through this challenge, you might get to the end and run out of motivation, dropping the activity. But if we build an effective system to get you there, then you aren't limited by our original goal.

We're going to ask you to write a couple things down, so please, cooperate, will you? We know it's a lot to ask, but this will actually help you a bunch. You want to have every advantage you can get, right?

We want to pair your meditation with an action you already do every day. It should be a habit that you already have, if possible, one that feels positive and useful to you. An example could be your first cup of coffee. Another example is brushing your teeth or arriving at the office. Pick an action that happens right before you want to meditate. Now, on a fresh piece of paper, or in your journal, write down, **"After I brush my teeth (or other habitual action), I will sit and meditate for one minute."** If this is your chosen action, then putting a note on the bathroom mirror saying, "Don't forget to meditate after you brush!" would be a good reminder.

You might have noticed that we asked you to write down one minute instead of five minutes. That's because this is the absolute minimum time investment, and if you can get to the cushion, then you can decide. Of course, we're really aiming for five to start.

For the best results, you need to put your statement of intention up where you will see it every day, or make it the lock screen on your phone, or write it on the back of your hand, whatever it takes to make sure you won't forget about it. That way, this will be an action you know you are going to do.

Every single time you succeed in sitting down to meditate, you need to congratulate yourself for following through. Clap your hands or smile and look up with a grin, or both! If you can find a chuckle in there, let it out. Remind yourself that you are accomplishing something big here. You have decided to do something for yourself, and you are following through because you have what it takes. This is the new you, and soon, you will use your new-found mental powers to accomplish who knows what!

Celebrate your little victory and go out into the world.

Key Takeaway Points From chapter 3

- Choose a location for meditating every day that is reasonably free of distractions
- Place items you will need in your location ahead of time - meditation pillow, cushions, timer, headphones, etc. so you will be ready without much effort
- Set an alarm to remind you of your appointment with the most important person in your life - you!
- Take a few moments ahead of time to determine your reasons for meditating, and journal or record these thoughts
- Do your best to anticipate and eliminate distractions - put your cell phone on "do not disturb," lock the door, ask others around you to leave you be, lock the children in the room their father is in (just kidding, dad - but this might work)

- Think about learning to enjoy the experience. Enter your session with the idea that you can train yourself to see meditation as relaxing and enjoyable. Remember that people tell themselves they like to wash dishes, and then they start liking that, so liking meditation should be way easier!
- If you miss a meditation session here or there, don't beat yourself up over it. Just do your very best to get the next one in. Don't let yourself miss three in a row! Imagine how upset you will be with yourself if you end up missing four meditations, and then just give up, and a year later, you find out that the rest of us are now all enlightened beings who no longer ever eat McDonald's food because we are too good for it. As you drag your butt through the golden arches, you will be very sorry that you didn't buckle down and do what you knew you should!
- Make a statement of intention, that says exactly when you will meditate. Put this statement on your bulletin board at

home or write it on someone forehead (kidding! Please don't d as they will be really mad, and also, they never hold still!), so you will see it and remember your intention to meditate
- Pair your meditation with an existing habit, such as immediately after your first cup of coffee or feeding the cat. The idea is that one habit will lead to the new one of meditating.

CHAPTER 4

THE 90-DAY SCHEDULE!

We hope that you already started day 1, and you are going to keep reading the book over the next few days, as you progress through the challenge. Check out the following sections to make sure you understand how we have the basic challenge set up, and then feel free to continue with the remainder of the chapters.

What If I Want To Meditate Longer?

This is totally in your court, it's your practice. But if you're a beginner, we suggest giving this routine a shot first and see what happens. Sitting for five minutes quietly can be challenging if you aren't used to it. There's no point in trying too hard at the beginning and losing interest because it's overwhelming and hard to stay put for the entire time you pick. It's best to choose a duration and sit through it no matter what, doing your best to stay mindful and follow the instructions.

If you are a little more practiced and you know you want to do more, then you should go ahead and sit for longer. You can modify the schedule as you need to, to get to 90 days.

I Want To Use A different Meditation That I Know Of. Can I Still Do The Challenge?

Our schedule uses a basic mindfulness, breath-focused meditation. We aren't saying this is the be all end all, ultimate meditation to use for everyone. If you've decided to use a different meditation, that's fine. For those who haven't meditated before, consider just giving the one here a chance, and you can switch it up later once you get your feet wet. In one of the upcoming chapters, we will be going over a few different meditation styles that we have used.

Days 1 to 10

Now we get into the thick of it. Here are the daily instructions to follow for the duration of the challenge. **We are going to start with five minutes, twice per day, for the first ten days.** This will get you used to the routine, and let you iron out any kinks you run into before you start sitting for longer times. As we talked about before, in the morning and near the end of the day would be optimum times, but we know this won't work for everyone. You might schedule for five minutes in the car at first coffee break out back behind the office, and at 5:00 PM while everyone else in your house is occupied with Netflix. Find your times and schedule it in!

1. Sit with your back in a neutral position. Don't sit on a soft chair or couch that has you leaning back, either sit cross-legged with a pillow lifting your butt or a stiff-backed chair. Tim uses an office chair in the locked position so it won't recline or a meditation cushion on top of a yoga mat. Don't worry about the lotus position; you don't need it! You want to be in a position

that's comfortable enough, you can maintain it for the duration of the timer. Also, if you will be crippled for days after sitting on the floor for five minutes, please don't do it! Use a chair! Learn from Tim's mistakes!

2. Take a few deep breaths and release them, just let the cares of the day slip away for a few minutes. You can start worrying again in five minutes! Put any devices on "Do Not Disturb" so no one will text you or send you an email and bother you. The world can wait for this brief time.

3. Set a timer on your phone or another device, double check to make sure it's running and set it aside. Tell yourself that you won't check to make sure it's still working, or to see how much longer. Of course it's running, you set it, right? Your job is to practice for the full five minutes.

4. Just watch your breath and feel it go in and out. You don't have to make it do anything. Just let it happen, and watch. Feel your chest rise, then fall. You could say "rise" to yourself on each intake of

breath, and then "fall" each time you breathe out.

5. If you lose track and then realize you aren't paying attention to your breaths, don't sweat it. Just start again. That's part of the process. You will go off on a tangent, maybe worrying if you got the instructions right, or remember that you need to pick up Johnny at 2:00, etc. Don't be hard on yourself, just get back to it and worry about Johnny after you're done here. He'll understand.

6. You might have an itch, or something, or feel like you need to fix your shirt. Some instructions tell you to suck it up and just sit there itching and all unadjusted. Our instructions say to go ahead and scratch the itch while paying deliberate attention to the act. Then go back to watching your breath. Remain as still as you can for the duration, and always wait for as long as possible before moving to fix your discomfort.

7. Keep going until that timer goes off. Stay with it no matter what! The only excuses for quitting early are: a crying baby that

you are only the caregiver for, a Roomba that repeatedly slams into you because you forgot to disable it beforehand, or being shot at by spies that are after the secret plans.

You might find yourself dozing off a bit or even passing right out. Don't be hard on yourself, just do your best to wake back up. If you have been pushed to the max and your body and soul desperately need that little break to de-stress and regenerate, then you're still doing yourself a favor. As you practice sitting every day, this should fade away, and you will be able to stay aware with concentration for longer periods.

Days 11 to 20

By now, your body and mind should be getting into the rhythm of the challenge. We hope you managed to practice twice a day for the last 10 days. And now, we are going to make it just a little bit tougher. You can follow the exact same instructions, and we are going to add… one minute.

That's right. **For days 11 through 20, practice sitting for 6 minutes, twice per day.** This small change should barely make any difference to the do-ability of the session. If you can do 5 minutes, 6 should be no problem.

To keep up your motivation to practice, it can be helpful to go back and review the earlier chapter on the benefits of meditation. Remember why you decided to take up this activity. Think about the sense of accomplishment you will have after completing this challenge. Think about how much you've already done! Getting as far as this is something many will never be able to do.

Remember to notice the peaceful and happy feelings in your body. Enjoy and savor the subtle sensations that you feel as you watch your breath come and go. Notice the tiny noises around you in your space, like the ticking of a clock or the gentle hum of the refrigerator. This will positively reinforce your mind to notice how much you are enjoying this experience.

Days 21 to 30

Add another minute to each session, for a total of 7 minutes, twice per day.

For most people, each time you practice will be a unique event. One day you will be a little sleepy and very relaxed, and maybe the next day almost unable to sit still with twitchy energy. As your mind starts to get used to these sessions, it might think it has it all figured out and start getting bored. This will lead to a period where you struggle to stay on your goal of mindful breathing. Your job is to just keep going anyway. If you feel yourself struggling, just relax again and notice everything around you. Be aware of your surroundings, your body, your breath, and your thoughts, all at the same time. This won't be easy, at first, but diligently train your mind to return to your breath while noticing your reality.

Days 31 to 40

Add another minute to each session, for a total of 8 minutes, twice per day.

At this point in the challenge, take a few minutes and reflect on the fact that you've meditated for a straight 30 days. Go you! Check in with your feelings about that; are you starting to feel the calmness and stillness as soon as you sit down to begin? Is the practice starting to seem like a normal activity for you? What are your biggest challenges with it? What are your biggest takeaways so far?

How does your body feel, before and then after meditations? Do you need to adjust how you are sitting to make it a more seamless experience? Have you determined what distractions are really driving you crazy, and learned how to deal with them? Have you made peace with that barking dog two neighbors over, so that he is now just part of the boiler room noises?

If you like to journal, jot down some notes and observations for your future reference. It will probably be interesting for you and help to remember how much different your perceptions of the experience used to be.

If you aren't yet a journaller, then pick up a pen and paper and give it a try!

Days 41 to 50

Add another minute to each session, for a total of 9 minutes, twice per day.

You might find that your meditation practice has become too predictable, and your mind is trying to get lazy. It knows what you are going to do: watch the breaths and maybe repeat the same word over and over. The subconscious mind might build a pattern to follow, so you don't have to do all this work anymore. And just like that, you're repeating that word automatically. No presence required. Now you can go back to thinking about Pinky and the Brain! Or replaying that encounter in the hallway at work where you dropped your lunch and embarrassed yourself in front of everyone. Or about how, in 10 minutes, you get to eat yogurt and a banana, and hot wings for supper! Yes!

This is where it can be helpful to switch things up a bit. Instead of just noticing the breath going in and out of your nose, notice how your chest rises and falls, for example. Then, count "one" for the first breath in. Now, continue counting each breath until you reach ten. At this point, count "nine" on the next breath in and work your way back to one. This will give your mind something to focus on and something to return to if you lose track. Whenever you find yourself replaying memories or thinking about what you're going to do once you get this darn sitting still over with, remember to start again with the breath.

Days 51 to 60

Just when you think you have us figured out, we go and fool you by adding... another minute, for 10 minutes twice per day.

Let's just imagine you, meditating, for a moment. There you are, sitting and breathing, and everything is going great. You're in the groove. The stars have aligned, and they are shining down on you with happiness. You are feeling good and noticing that you feel good.

This is when your subconscious will toss something out there to distract you, and hopefully get you off your butt, working on its stuff instead. You might suddenly remember that you need to text Linda and let her know that she has to meet you at 1:00. You imagine the text: "Listen, Linda. Meet me at 1:00 by the front door of the mall." If you don't jump up and do this right now, you will definitely forget. The temptation to grab your phone and text Linda will be like a physical pain.

The only reason you aren't going to do it is you will remember that you read how this exact thing was going to happen. So now that we warned you, you know that you have to wait until that timer goes off to text Linda.

Ok, where were you? Right. You were paying attention to your breath. And you were noticing how your body feels. There, back on track. "But what about Linda?" part of you wails. Don't worry. Linda will still be there in a few minutes. This is all about you time. This isn't time for Linda or texting.

Unless your name is Linda. If it is, then this time is all about Linda. But still not about texting.

Days 61 to 70

This time we really are going to fool you and add 2 minutes, for a total of 12 minutes, twice per day.

If adding more time isn't working for you, then just stick with 10 minutes (or even five.) You will be better off if you work at maintaining 5 minutes, or 10 minutes, instead of getting frustrated and dropping the whole practice because you are feeling frustrated and unable to sit still. You can always work at increasing the time later. For now, the most important thing is making it to day 90 and building that habit.

Two months in. Amazing! You should be feeling some pretty good effects by this point and a sense of satisfaction at making it this far. Hopefully, you are leaving the cushion with a sense of calmness, ready for the world. Examine how you are feeling about meditation, and how you feel before and after each session. Journal your feelings, like before, for future reference.

Days 71 to 80

Increase your time to 15 minutes, twice per day.
Remember to check in with your body, notice any pleasant sensation, enjoy the stillness. As you feel your breath, listen for the tiny noises of the curtain fluttering by the open window, or the muted footsteps of the neighbor in the next apartment over. Can you hear or feel the movement of any air around you?

Days 81 to 90

Now we are in the big time. **Increase your sitting time to 20 minutes, twice per day.**
Remember: this time period is just a suggestion. Each person is different. Feel free to adjust this as required, maybe you still feel that 5 or 6 minutes is where you need to be. Or maybe you are ready and want to try 30 minutes. Do what will work for you.

Wow, you're really doing this! Only a few days to go, and you will be one of those rare meditation people that are spoken of in hushed tones, looked up to by the masses, revered for their determination, and feared for their superhuman ability to ignore the fact that their elbow is so super itchy for, like, ten minutes straight. You are indeed among the blessed.

Finish Line - Celebrate!

We are so proud of you for making it all the way to the end of this challenge! Woohoo! You are one awesome human! Bring it in for a hug!

Some studies show that two or three months of meditation can give you 60% of the physical benefits of meditation practice. This means that, right now, you will have already achieved 60% of the peace of mind and stress reduction that is possible to get out of meditation practice. Your heart, your circulation system, your immune system will be thanking you big time right about now. Personal relationships are feeling the benefits, too. All you have to do, to hang on to these benefits, is to keep up your practice, so you don't slip back down the hill. Stick with it, so you don't slide back into the muddy pit of the normals, the untrained non-meditators who are

60% more stressed than you. You don't want that, so keep meditating!

Key Takeaway Points From chapter 4

- You can adjust the length of your meditation sessions as you feel you need to, but we ask that you make them at least 5 minutes long. If you feel like you can do more, go ahead! If you feel that you need to keep the sessions the same length for the entire 90 days, that might be right for you. Just remember that you may not be in the same place with 5-minute-long sessions as you would with longer ones.
- If you want to try using a different meditation than the one we suggest starting with, then go ahead, but we suggest giving the mindfulness breath meditation a try first.
- Days 1 to 10: 5 minutes, twice a day
- Days 11 to 20: 6 minutes, twice a day
- Days 21 to 30: 7 minutes, twice a day
- Days 31 to 40: 8 minutes, twice a day
- Days 41 to 50: 9 minutes, twice a day

- Days 51 to 60: 10 minutes, twice a day
- Days 61 to 70: 12 minutes, twice a day
- Days 71 to 80: 15 minutes, twice a day
- Days 81 to 90: 20 minutes, twice a day
- Victory! You are now 60% of the way to being superhuman! Your saga will be the stuff legends are made of. When they write about the meditation revolution that swept the earth and started the era of much less stressed humans, you will be in that story. Sit tall with happiness as you keep going with your meditation habit!

CHAPTER 5

USING A CALENDAR

You're almost set to really take this the distance. But how will you keep track of where you are on this journey to 90 days of awesome mind-expanding practice, to know when it's complete? How will you know which days you missed and which day is day 30, time to go to phase three?

There are a few ways to log your practice and keep motivation up at the same time. The key to making it work is to keep it simple enough that it doesn't take long to use, and convenient enough that it doesn't take much effort. We all have a ton of things drawing on our attention and willpower, so we definitely don't need yet another time sink sidetracking us. Again, planning just a little right off the bat will make a huge difference to whether or not you reach the finish line. Before we get to some options, let's look at the basic streak method.

The Streak Method

You might be able to guess from the title that we are going to go for a winning streak of days or events, where you keep up the intensity level and build your new habit by showing up for every session. When you look at the record you're keeping, you get a sense of accomplishment, and as you check off each step of the journey, your subconscious mind cheers at the progress. This method is reportedly the key to the success of comedian Jerry Seinfeld, who used it to track his joke writing efforts.

Jerry's advice to another hopeful comedian was to get a wall calendar with every day of the year on it and hang it up where he could see it every day. Then, each day after successfully writing a joke, take a red felt marker and put a big "X" on the day. Mr. Seinfeld's final piece of advice was "don't break the chain."

An interesting point to take from this is that he never said "funny" joke. It could be a total groaner or even depressing. The important thing was to write it, and to cross off the day, never breaking the chain.

We want to sit and meditate every day, and form a winning streak or chain of days, to build a habit and make a lifestyle change. We do want to follow instructions and accomplish the work, but the biggest hurdle is simply showing up, sitting there for the entire time, and logging our session. This is more important to the process than whether or not you spent three minutes worrying about your daughter's first date, or how Tony Stark could possibly defeat Thanos now that his suit is ruined, and he's stranded in outer space. Maybe you are sitting, and everything seems to go sideways. Your mind totally squirrels on you, your left foot is itchy, and you want ice cream. It's okay, you can sit through all of that for just a few minutes. The joke doesn't have to be funny, but you do have to write it to keep up the streak!

As you go through the challenge and build a chain, the sense of accomplishment will be there, but even more importantly, you will be exercising your willpower muscles. While training your brain to sit and practice, you will also be expanding the important part of you that not only knows it can get stuff done but has the gumption to dig in and do the work. This is a huge deal! It will overflow into other areas of your life and help you get stuff done there too.

Imagine this new focus letting you keep up the motivation for that personal project that you have been putting off. It seems likely that one reason meditators are usually more creative than they would be without the practice of being mindful is that they have an increased amount of get-off-the-couch power. They were always able to do the thing, they just didn't before. Now, they find the ability inside themselves to focus and move forward.

Paper Calendars

Like Jerry Seinfeld suggested, a wall calendar would be an excellent way to keep track of a streak of winning behavior. You could write the challenge at the top to keep it in mind, highlight day 1 and the ending day, and keep a marker nearby to go through the days. It wouldn't have to be a calendar with every day on one big page, it could be a regular monthly calendar.

A big advantage to the paper calendar could be that it is a highly visible item, something you will see every day and will remind you to do the thing. A disadvantage could be that everyone else you live with will also see it, and if you aren't interested in their input, you won't want them having access to your personal log of meditation.

If you are making a small shrine or meditation altar, your calendar could be above it. You can get some amazing calendars, with pictures of almost anything on them. Pick something uplifting and inspiring, or just pick kittens/puppies. Alternatively, if sharks are your thing, a nice shark calendar will do the trick.

Since we are doing two sessions per day, if you are marking a calendar, draw one part of the "X" each time you sit. That way you can track whether or not you completed both of your sessions, or just one, or if you are missing that day completely.

Journal

A regular journal or notebook can be a great way to track your 90-Day Meditation Challenge. Maybe you already have a journal and use it every day, in which case, you can easily write "Meditation Challenge Day 5" or whatever day you are on, in the top corner of your journal. If you don't have a journal or notebook, it's a great opportunity; go get one!

This is the method Tim typically uses to keep track of all kinds of things, such as how many days in a row he did yoga. For journaling ideas, check out the internet and do a couple searches for "journal layouts." Just be prepared to spend a bit of time looking around at everyone's carefully crafted pages with jealousy and the desire to copy everything you see!

Keeping a journal for the challenge would also give you the opportunity to make some notes about your meditation practice. If you write down your thoughts and a little bit about the experience, you can review this later for insights. You might find, for instance, that there are certain distractions that are a huge challenge for you time and again. Or that those distractions were a huge problem, but no longer bother you as much. The journal would be a good way to see the progress you've made and any difficulties you overcame.

Alternatively, you can use one page in your journal as a habit tracker in the style of a bullet journal layout. For this method, you will put the boxes for each day in a line beside the habit you're tracking and fill in a box each time you complete the task. This can be a fun way to keep track, depending on your personality and likes.

If you like journaling and you like stickers, a fun way to keep track is to pick up some stickers from the dollar store or craft store. Every day that you follow through on your practice, place a sticker on the page. You could get happy faces or unicorns, or even Superman stickers.

Smartphone Apps

No matter which app we mention right now, it's a sure bet that there will be several more on the market by the time you read this. Smartphone apps have come a long way, with more features and uses all the time. If you like the idea of tracking your challenge with an app, there's a lot of options to help you.

Many of these apps are based on the streak method and contain the word "streak" in their name. They track how many days in a row you complete a task, provided you remember to open the app and mark the action complete.

The big benefit to these apps is portability. You will already have your phone with you, so marking the meditation as complete is easy to do. If you are going to practice in the car before work, for example, you don't necessarily want to be packing a calendar or journal around.

Another benefit to the app is reminders and scheduling. The app could send you a notification to remind you to meditate, a really useful feature if you might forget.

There are also meditation apps out there that help you with guided meditations if you want to check them out. Headspace is one of the most popular of these mindfulness apps at the time we wrote this book. If you decide to use a meditation app on a daily basis, you can still count this as part of the 90-day challenge. We won't hold it against you, we promise.

Our Custom Calendar

We also have a downloadable calendar for you to use, free of charge. This 90-day one-page challenge calendar can be printed off and put in your planner, on the fridge, used as a bookmark, kept in the bathroom by the mirror, or wherever you like. It's standard letter size, 8.5" by 11," for easy home printing. If you would like this calendar, go to www.tim-ebl.com and get your free pdf.

This calendar is, of course, the best option. Just because it's ours, and we made it. That's why, without taking into account your personal preferences or the fact that we quickly whipped up an excel sheet calendar, you should just go with this option. Did we mention it's free? And did we mention it comes with a 90-Day Meditation Challenge Guide? Did we mention that's also free? We think you should definitely get it.

Key Takeaway Points From Chapter 5

- **The Streak Method can give you a way to keep track of any activity you want to and helps you gamify the activity so you can try to make it into a habit. The goal is to mark down having meditated every day, every session, with an unbroken streak. And remember, every joke you write doesn't have to be funny, but you have to write it. Every meditation session doesn't have to feel successful, but you have to show up and sit!**
- **An old-fashioned calendar or paper journal can be the easiest way to keep**

track of the 90-Day Meditation Challenge. If you like stickers, markers, and journals, make all these things a part of your day.
- Smartphone apps can be a useful way to remind yourself to meditate, as well as keeping track of it when you do sit. You can even use some apps to guide you through a meditation.
- We have a free gift for you! It includes a one-page calendar that you can use to keep track, so go to www.timebl.com/bonus to access it.

CHAPTER 6

SUPPORT SYSTEM

How to Succeed - Part of a Team

So now you have a general background of why meditation is so healthy for your entire being, and a template to get started on the 90-day challenge. You have a few options to pick for keeping track of the days and to help stay focused. You could probably get the job done on your own, but why not take advantage of any support that you can get from the outside world? It can be tough to stay motivated at the best of times, so to increase the odds of making it to day 90, we recommend slanting the odds in your favor as much as possible. Here are a few ideas to keep up the streak!

Family or Friends

You might be one of those lucky individuals who has a huge support group of family or friends, who are on your side and support you with anything you do. Or even just one family member or friend that has your back. If this is you, consider talking to them about this challenge and enlisting their aid in keeping motivated. This is called an accountability partner or buddy, and it can be a really helpful way to keep going when things get tough.

If you can find a person in your life to bring in on your goal of meditating for 90 days, and then make a plan to communicate with them periodically through the challenge, you will be more likely to follow through on your plans. They might not be interested in meditating themselves, but that's okay, as long as they are willing to give you a hand. Your partner needs to be willing to helping you succeed. If the person you have in mind is wishy-washy about it at all, don't involve them in the process. They might have the opposite effect of that intended and end up demotivating you.

Buddy System

The buddy system is exactly like the accountability partner, except this person also does the challenge alongside you. If you are able to sit together, you will have an automatic accountability check to ensure you stay on the cushion for the entire time set on the timer!

While it would work the absolute best if you were in the same physical location and practiced at the same time, this will most likely be impractical due to distance and schedule. Texts or emails could be your means of communication. This partner would be a great sounding board for your successes, any issues that arise, and an all-around great motivator to keep up the challenge. Human beings are social creatures and having a friend to share the journey with makes everything better.

You might not have anyone like that in your life, but here are a couple ideas to find a buddy to meditate with. Do you go to a yoga class or work out with anyone at the gym? These are the ideal types of people to approach with the idea of meditation because they are already investing in their wellbeing on a weekly basis. This person is going to be more open to the idea than a random work acquaintance who spends way too much time on Netflix.

Still stuck finding a buddy? Check out our Facebook page.

Facebook Page

We have created a Facebook group to help everyone out with tips and tricks, positive messages, inspirational quotes, and videos. We will also be letting people post there to look for a meditation buddy. And of course, the entire community will support your 90-day meditation goal. For anyone who is struggling to find someone to talk to about meditation and that side of their lives, we encourage you to join our community group at www.facebook.com/groups/90DayMeditationChallenge/

Website

We may have mentioned Tim's website a couple of times. There will be info there about the

Facebook page, as well as other news and updates which might be helpful.

Key Takeaway Points From Chapter 6

- You can multiply your chances of getting through this challenge if you have the support of at least one person. They don't have to meditate with you, they just need to be supportive and curious.
- The best support you could get is a partner who will do the challenge with you. You might know someone from your life that you can ask. Make sure if you pick a partner to sit with, that they are actually the type of person that follows through!
- If you want a partner but don't know anyone, all is not lost. You can go to our Facebook page for help with finding a meditation partner. They won't sit with you in person, but it can be just as effective to have an accountability partner online.

- You can also go to www.Tim-Ebl.com to check for any updates on support for a meditation partner if you don't use Facebook. Some of the information will be posted there too.

CHAPTER 7

THE BODY AND MEDITATION

The Yoga Connection

If you are new to meditation and yoga, you might be a bit confused about the way the two are entangled. As we mentioned before, the body movements of yoga are designed to prepare the practitioner for sitting and meditation. While a full yoga practice would be the best way to get the benefits, Kyla has a simple primer that can help you get yourself out of the way of your body. This section can be useful to everyone, no matter what your starting point is. Here are her thoughts on body preparation, and a way to gain more awareness. We will not be going into a full yoga routine, just some simplified stretches and breath exercises. We encourage you to go past this introduction and take a more extensive foray into yoga - but in your own time! Don't derail your 90-Day Meditation Challenge by wandering off and signing up for a whole bunch of yoga instead.

Kyla's Body Awareness and Tension Relieving Breath Primer

Preparing the body for meditation is the truest aspect of physical yoga. The ancient seekers would sit for meditation and realize that the discomfort in their bodies would bring action to the mind. It's told that they began to observe the animals that surround them, and it was noticed that in the natural world, the beasts would honor their bodies by stretching. They observed birds stretching their wings, cats arching their backs. You may have noticed that your dog naturally does the yoga position Down Dog. Over the course of my career, I have met many people that feel their clever K9 companion has decided to do yoga. The truth is, yogis stole it from the dog.

Yoga, the physical practice, was developed to relieve the physical body of the effects of gravity and release the trapped emotions of the body. This is a far cry from the monstrosity of Western yoga and the idea that change occurs from the outside, when in fact, we wish to create inner space with asana (yoga posture). It's like a massage from the inside out. When yoga is approached in this way, the personal change comes from inside. The tension and stress are released from the core of the being. It is not to be forced or pushed, but accepted and allowed, to use this connection in creating a dialog of acceptance between both the mind and the body. The practice of meditation is to develop the ability to sit as one, both mind and body. This, in turn, affects our emotional state of being. This is also different from the Western idea of meditation being totally cut off from reality, unaware of what is going on around you or in your body.

But why is it so very hard in the beginning? From birth, most of us are not taught that we can master the mind and its thoughts. We are trained that the world is outside ourselves. The longer we live like this, the more the mind begins to believe that it "knows." We go through life, and we collect experiences, and this brings the mind to a space where it feels it "knows" what to expect. The longer we live in this space of untrained mind, the more the world seems to be predictable to the mind, and we collect "truths" of our experience. "Life is hard work" or "I am unlovable." When we try to sit in meditation, the mind begins to regurgitate everything it thinks it "knows."

You see, the mind feels it is keeping us safe in this space. Alert... Thinking. Assessing and judging what is happening as a "good" experience or a "bad" experience. When the mind is silent and connected to the body, it is forced to connect with the experiences we are carrying and the tension of our thoughts that is stored in the body.

Your nervous system is the point of origin for all aspects of self. Each cortex and area of the mind are directly related to various areas of the body. So in turn, when we affect the body, this directly brings electrical current to specific areas of the mind and brain. This will trigger thoughts held in the specific cortex. Yoga poses are meant to create this experience, and the practice is to see if we can find peace in them. We meet the tension with breath, grace, and acceptance, in both the mind and body.

It has been my experience that an effective way to pacify the mind is through the waves of the breath. The mind softens when it is met with rich oxygenation, and when the mind softens, so does the body. It gives the mind something physical and pleasurable to experience, slowly coaxing the mind into a released state.

Tension in the Face, Neck, and Shoulders Reduces Brain Capacity!

Muscle tension in the face, neck, and shoulders has a great effect on the amount of oxygen provided to the brain. When we are tense in these areas and restrict oxygen, it causes the neurons of mind to frantically fire, increasing thoughts. Not only do the tense muscles require more blood flow for themselves, but they reduce the flow to the overactive brain. Subconsciously, we are fighting for air. This keeps us in the fight or flight response and tense throughout the entire body. If you are to prepare any part of the body for meditation, it is best to release here.

Releasing the Spine

According to yoga, the strength and structure of the spine greatly affect our physical and mental health. Each section of the spine has branches of nerves that service different groups of organs. Releasing spine tension allows for more natural and consistent electrical currents to stimulate the internal organs and intestines, and this allows them to work more efficiently.

Releasing Tension in the Hips and Legs

Yoga shows us that tension in the hips and legs is reflective of how we feel about and move through life. You might have heard that the hips are like the body's junk drawer, where any leftover "stuff" ends up. Loose hips and legs allow us to move gracefully through the day-to-day, creating space for us to be more accepting of life and our journey in it.

Breathing, You're Already a Winner!

The trick is to become conscious of the breath, aware of each inhalation and exhalation. At first, the mind will shy away from this connection, as it feels the body has it handled, and this interrupts the mind from its duties of keeping you safe. You see the mind become accustomed to its noise, and the silence can be a very scary place. Using a natural rhythm of the body allows for a natural process to take place. Over time, it will become so natural that a couple of mindful breaths will soften and center the mind very quickly. With enough practice, mindfulness can arrive very quickly.

How we breathe affects the direction of energy into our body. For instance, if you are running, the best way to supply oxygen to the body is through the mouth. This feeds the energy into the heart and lungs. Very useful to outrun a lion. In meditation, the objective is to feed the mind oxygen. So it is very useful to breathe through the nostrils. Directing the energy to the mind, oxygenating and softening the firing of the neurons.

From Head to Toe or Toe to Head

We will give the directions from head to toe, but as we have stated, meditation is a personal journey, and you may have more success going from toe to head. We encourage you to play freely and sort out what is best for you. Meditation is a personal recipe for all of us, and it is important to not put ourselves or the practice in another box of "I am." Things will change, and you will grow. Your practice will grow with you.

Take a second form seated or standing: Close your eyes and take a deep breath, see if you can feel the oxygen pass the nostrils. Use your senses and feel the cool air enter your body. See if you can follow its journey. Feel it pass over the mind and come cool into the throat and then the lungs. See if you can notice your chest full of breath. Good! This is all you need as we begin to enter our bodies and prepare for meditation.

1. Continue drawing the breath in through the nostrils, let the cool inhalation rise deep into the chest and relax the body as the breath leaves. Notice how, as you fill

the chest, it brings a natural extension to the spine. No need to force it, as the breath does all the work. Watch the inhalations and exhalations as though you are watching waves come and go from a beach. Let the chest expand and fill with oxygen. Your body is the beach, and with each wave that comes, it changes the beach ever so slightly. Do this five times.

2. As you watch a wave of breath rise into the chest, with the exhalation, release the tension of your face. Let the eyes roll into the head, release the jaw and let the tongue rest in the mouth. Take three breaths, and with each exhalation, release the tension of the face.

3. We move to the neck. Continue to breathe into the body. Feel your chest rise and with an exhalation bring your chin to the chest. As you inhale, allow the pressure of the breath to rise into the chest as high as you can to deepen the stretch into the back of the neck. As the wave of breath leaves the body, release the muscles of the neck, and let the muscles of the face

soften to the earth with gravity. Deep breaths into the neck and allow it all to soften. Do this five times. We will bring some motion into the stretch. Breathe deeply into the back of the neck, and with an exhalation, softly roll the right ear to the right shoulder. Inhale deeply into the side of the neck and then relax the face, tongue, and shoulders with the exhalation. (Only moving with the exhalations.) Take one more nice deep breath through the nostrils, and like a dance with the exhalation, softly roll the left ear to the left shoulder. Expand your body with the inhalation. Big breath into the side of the neck, and once again, release the muscles of the face, neck, and shoulders with the exhalation. Make three more rounds ending on the left-hand side.

4. Continue making space in the neck, shoulders, and chest. As you bring a deep breath into your chest, draw your shoulders as close to your ears as you can, with the exhalation, bring the shoulders back in and down.

5. Making movement in the spine. You can be sitting or standing, it is up to you. We are simply releasing the tension stored in the spine. As you fill your lungs and widen the rib cage, a natural extension of the spine occurs. Bring the breath wide into the rib cage, and then, with the exhalation, look deep over your right shoulder. Allow the head to lead as it looks over the right shoulder, and then the extension of the spine follows. Squeezing the air out as you twist, there is no need to force it - allow it to happen naturally. With the inhalation, return to center. Let the spine get long, and then, with the exhalation, look to the left, and allow the spine to flow, squeezing the air out as you twist to the left. Return to center with the inhalation and repeat three times.

6. Legs, hips, and lower back. Depending on your flexibility, you may require support. Remember, this is supposed to be an enjoyable experience. Please honor your body at all times, and do not do anything that causes physical stress. We are here to

release stress, and you have the rest of the day to collect it if you so wish. But for now, we do what feels good. From standing or sitting, take a big breath into your chest and let your spine be strong and long, raise your arms out in front at shoulder height and shoulder width apart. As you exhale, bend forward bringing your hands to a chair or to the floor. If you are halfway between the chair and the floor, find something that is the right height to support you. Yoga blocks, books, a stool, get creative in finding your support. Once you are in your forward fold, feel your feet, and have even pressure between the ball and the heel of the foot. This may affect the depth of your bend. It's more important to find balance than depth in the pose. As you continue to make space in the body with the breath, breathe deeply into the back of the shoulders. Let the breath expand you, and as you exhale, relax your shoulders, neck, and face. Continue to expand like a big balloon, and as you release the breath, relax again. Let the

shoulders sink toward the ears, and the neck and face to let go. Do this five times and then return to standing. Once standing, take three more breaths deeply into the chest, let your spine extend and your rib cage open.
7. **Please note:** at any time, if you feel congested in your chest after an exercise, release the breath through the mouth. In through the nose and out through the mouth.

Your body is now prepared to release and let go in meditation. Enjoy your loose muscles as you begin.

Releasing Tension for Those With Limited Mobility

Yoga or meditation, contrary to Western concept, truly is for everyone. We just do what we can with what we have. If you feel that the program above may be too much for your body, we offer you this alternative. It is still important to draw the focus of the mind to the body pre-meditation, even if you have limited mobility.

Meditation and yoga are for everyone. I once had a student that used a wheelchair, with almost no movement in her body. We would do the following exercises to prepare for our meditation classes.

From a lying position, head slightly raised by a cushion.

1. As you inhale, tightly squeeze the muscles of your face. Like you have bitten into a lemon. As you exhale, allow the face to release and relax. The eyes roll into the head, keep the tongue loose in the back of the mouth, jaw relaxed. Repeat three times.
2. Now move into the arms and shoulders but keep engaging the squeeze in the face. As you breathe deeply into your chest, make tight fists, squeeze your arm muscles, and bring your shoulders to your ears all in one motion. Big breaths. Squeeze everything as tight as you can and then let it go. Timing the release with your exhalation. Let the face release, Let

the shoulders relax, the arms let go, and the hands relax. Repeat three times.

3. We continue to move through the body. With the next three breaths, we engage all the body parts from before, and this time, include the torso and buttocks. As you inhale, bring conscious tension to the face, shoulders, arms, hands, torso, and buttocks. With the wave of exhalation, let it all go. Repeat three times.

4. We now bring the legs and feet in for a full body squeeze, from the face to the toes. With an inhalation, squeeze the entire body tight, tight, tight, and then let go from the face to the feet. Big, deep breaths. Squeeze it all in an let it all go. Repeat five times, and take a few breaths resting in the relaxed body you have created.

CHAPTER 8

ALTERNATIVE MEDITATIONS AND SYSTEMS, AND FINDING A TEACHER

Why You Should Consider A Teacher and Further Training

If you think about meditation like a gym for your mind, why you need some guidance will make a lot of sense. Imagine an out of shape fellow named James who wants to look like one of his favorite superheroes from the movies, with impressive rippling muscles and an extra thick neck. He goes into a gym near his work, asks for a membership, and tells them he doesn't need the introductory visit with the complimentary personal trainer. He has decided he can figure out this gym business on his own! How hard can it be? This isn't his first rodeo. He did read that one book on weight training. He signs the waiver form and gets busy, just like a hamster in a wheel.

So James starts going to the gym twice a week. He begins using various random isolation machines, a few dumbbells, and he walks on the treadmill. He has no plan, he isn't consistent, and his form is terrible. He doesn't realize he is hurting himself until he gets tennis elbow so badly that he can't even barely move his right arm. Right on, James!

Meditation can be just like the gym. Aimlessly wandering around in your own skull won't necessarily help you in the long run.

Consider this book like the complimentary visit with the personal trainer. Our job is to show you around a bit, teach a few basic moves, and go over basic safety. Show you where the changing rooms and showers are, how to hold a dumbbell over your head without dropping it on your skull, things like that. And of course, give you a basic workout plan, which is the 90-day Meditation Challenge.

You could absolutely benefit from some more guidance, and there are plenty of places to get help with meditation in every major population center.

Be wary of experimenting with various techniques you read about online without some help and supervision! We are just asking you use your common sense when you consider focusing hard on your third eye while breathing in a certain way for extended periods, just because some one-page website explained that this would give you animal telepathy. It's unlikely that you will hurt yourself, but also likely that you will be disappointed in your lack of ability to read your dog Woofie's mind after months of hard work.

Alternative Meditations

It could be that the breath-focused meditation just doesn't seem to be a good fit for you, and you might want a different method to try. Here is a quick breakdown of some of the types of meditation out there, although, this by no means an exhaustive list or description. If you read about one of these and decide to explore it further, please do a bit of research before diving right in. We will give some basic instructions here to give you a basic idea of how these methods are used.

Object Focused Meditation

In this type of practice, the meditator uses an external physical item, such as a rock or coin, to focus the mind. The object should be big enough to see easily, and small enough to fit inside your frame of vision so that you don't have to move your head around to see the entire thing.

The meditator might first calm the mind with breath-focused meditation, and then open his or her eyes to observe the chosen item. The idea would be to take in every detail, the way the light falls on it, how rough or smooth it is, and not make any judgments or associations about it. Attempting to see the object for what it is without interpreting it will lead to fewer thoughts and increase the ability of the mind to concentrate. As with the breath meditation, when you have a lapse in concentration, then you gently return to the object without being upset with yourself.

For this meditation, you could use a flower, candle flame, a picture, a rock, or a statuette. It should be in clear view, so you don't have to strain to see it.

Some use natural items, such as trees, while sitting outside on a deck or by a walking path. From a stress-reducing point of view, sitting in nature observing a tree, boulder, or stream seems ideal. Weather permitting, of course. Focused object meditation in nature sounds like a great way to spend some time!

Visualization

Visualization is a kind of meditation where you focus on an image or scene in your imagination. This is different from focusing on your breath or a repeated word/phrase, as both these meditation methods have the effect of reducing or slowing down the stream of images flashing through most people's heads, while visualization asks you to control or place images there instead.

A guided visualization uses an audio track to guide you through an imagined scene or scenes, usually with the expected benefits of relaxation and stress reduction. While these guided visualizations have their uses, they aren't the same as the traditional sitting meditation practice, and they aren't expected to give you the same benefits of personal insight, etc. They can calm the mind and body and are definitely useful for many people who aren't interested or ready for another meditation form.

A mental rehearsal of a sports move or event is one visualization widely used by athletes to improve their performance in everything from golf shots to football throws and catches, to motocross jumps. While resting in a relaxed position, the athlete mentally runs through the actions they will need to complete their event, visualizing in great detail a perfect swing, throw, or jump. This type of visualization is in use by football players, Olympic athletes, race car drivers, basically all serious competitors. Even world-class poker players have been known to use this technique to improve their game.

In Tim's book, Demons in The Cellar, he wrote about a very specific form of visualization intended to reduce the lingering stress and trauma of extremely bad memories. The basic concept is to revisit the memory, playing it through a couple times as it happened. Then, make slight changes to the outcome of the memory to reduce its impact. For example, if you have a terrible memory of being humiliated in the office lunchroom by James, you would imagine that James had a sudden wardrobe malfunction right before the altercation starts. For more information on this technique, please check out his previous book. It is a very effective way to move on from all kinds of traumatic events by reframing the outcomes. The original memory still exists, of course, but as you use the technique repeatedly, it becomes blunted.

Mantras

You may have heard of mantras and wondered exactly what they were, and why everyone talks about them. The word gets misused a lot, referring to the unconscious repetition of a phrase, or pounding a specific saying into your head. "Why 'More money!' Must Become Your Mantra!", one internet article proclaims. "It was like his mantra, he just kept repeating 'They are going to pay for the wall.'"

Mantra is a Sanskrit word, which, roughly translated, means 'tool to free the mind.' It consists of a word or phrase that is intended to be spoken aloud, spoken silently, or listened to. While there might be a meaning to the words, traditionally, they were used for the sound or vibration quality that it was intended to create in the person speaking/ listening to the mantra.

Similar to the way music or other vibrations can change your mood and thinking, the intention of the mantra was also partly to affect your mind through vibrational quality. As the mantra is repeated over and over in a carefully attentive way, the sound is expected to embed itself in your mind. The repetition slowly builds to a critical mass, where the effect of each additional iteration adds to the last.

Another effect that a mantra can have is to briefly replace your regular thoughts, basically "talking over" your busy mind chatter. Every time you say your mantra out loud or in your head, you are forced to take a break from thinking about those special brownies your cousin promised to bake next Tuesday at 4:20, and just say the word or phrase. Shutting your internal dialog for that moment can let your brain drag the scattered attention bits into a pile and focus for a change.

There are many resources to find mantras online, and it's quite a common meditation method taught everywhere. The book "Success Through Stillness," by Russell Simmons and Chris Morrow, teaches a basic meditation technique using a mantra that is similar to the Transcendental Meditation Technique used by the authors.

A very basic mantra is one we already mentioned, to say "rise" each time you take in a breath, and "fall" every time you breathe out. It works best if at first you say the word out loud to yourself, and then over time, only whisper the mantra. Only ever saying the words in your head will take much longer for this technique to bear fruit.

While you can pick a mantra on your own from a website or book, this is a technique that could definitely benefit from time spent with a mentor.

Walking Meditation

> *"Take short steps in complete relaxation; go slowly with a smile on your lips, with your heart open to an experience of peace."*
> *- Thich Nhat Hanh*

Walking meditations are a form of active meditation that takes place while walking at a slower pace than normal. The goal is not to arrive or to get somewhere. The purpose is to move mindfully and increase concentration. Steps are coordinated with breathing, mantras, and practices. The resulting experience can be as deep as a seated meditation and has the added benefit of giving you a break from all that stationary sitting!

To try out walking meditation, you don't need a lot of space; a large room, hallway, or back yard would suffice. If you're planning on walking in public, make sure you won't be going where there's heavy traffic or a lot of pedestrian congestion. There are a couple reasons, the first being safety, and the second being you will probably feel uncomfortable with so many eyes on you, at least at first.

Once you've found a safe, undisturbed area with minimal distractions, stand still for a few moments, and feel the weight of your body pressing your feet into the ground. Feel your body balance against gravity, become present in your body. Take a few deep breaths, and with your eyes closed, check out how you're feeling inside and out. Be aware of your physical self and where it is in the surrounding area.

The easiest form of walking meditation to try is a mindfulness form that has the practitioner pay attention to the entire experience. Feeling your feet touching the ground, notice your footwear and how it fits. Feel the movements of your body and muscles and try to move with grace and ease at a slow pace. Be with your motion and notice each step. Keep your attention on your mental processes and thoughts as you move and follow the same steps as in sitting meditations. If your attention wanders to what's around the corner or what the jogger coming toward you is going to think, as soon as you notice that your thoughts are off target, then gently return to the awareness of your foot touching down.

As you step, you could count to help keep your focus. Count one on the first step, then two on the second step, all the way to ten. Then start back at one.

A great source of information for this practice is the book Walking Meditation: Easy Steps to Mindfulness by Thich Nhat Hanh and Nguyen Anh-Huong. If you want to work on a practice of meditation that you can use anywhere from nature to your home to busy city streets, then this is a must read. The authors go through the breathing and mindfulness you will need to progress as a meditative walker.

Transcendental Meditation

The Transcendental Meditation Technique is a popular system that uses a silent mantra while sitting with your eyes closed for 15 to 20 minutes at a session. To learn this meditation form, you need to pay a certified instructor and take the course. Transcendental Meditation is used by a lot of people worldwide, and practitioners claim that it has changed their lives.

The list of celebrities and famous people who use Transcendental Meditation every day is huge. Here are a few that you might recognize, and this is by no means a complete list of famous endorsers: Tim Ferriss, Tom Hanks, Jennifer Lopez, David Lynch, Cameron Diaz, Russel Brand, Hugh Jackman, Sheryl Crow, Liv Tyler, and Katy Perry.

Maybe some of their success is due to their meditation habits? It's hard to say which came first. And of course, some of them took up meditating after they made the big time. But in the case of a famous director, such as David Lynch, his 40-plus-year meditation habit suggests that it's a good influence on his creativity.

The David Lynch Foundation is an organization that was started to "ensure that every child anywhere in the world who wanted to learn to meditate could do so." This is a very worthy goal, and it shows how much David Lynch thinks meditation practice is worth. There is a lot of good information at their site, www.davidlynchfoundation.org.

To learn this form of meditation, a simple internet search will give you local instructors that can teach you. Be prepared for the price tag! While this isn't the cheapest course to take, it might pay back huge dividends in personal growth through a lifetime, and it definitely seems to be making a huge impression on thousands of users who promote it.

Loving Kindness Meditation

This type of practice is especially good at helping to foster positive emotions and happiness, which you can take with you everywhere in life. On top of that, it has many of the stress-relieving and health benefits of other meditation styles. The practitioner focuses on cultivating thoughts and feelings of compassion for him or herself and then others. This might be done by repeating a phrase like "May I be well and Happy." You wish yourself happiness and try to actually feel the feelings of joy and compassion.

Next, you move on to people who are close to you, that you admire and like already. You wish them happiness and health in the same way, doing your best to bring up the actual feelings.

Now you can move on to people you know that you are neutral toward, again wishing them happiness. This can be acquaintances, the cashier at the grocery store, your neighbor, etc.

Next, you wish strangers and those you don't know health and happiness. You could imagine this as a widening circle that radiates love and compassion, or you could think of specific strangers you know of, etc.

The final stage of this form of meditation is the most challenging. Here, you think of people that you don't like, and you wish them health and happiness. It can be challenging to find feelings of compassion and happiness for people that don't make your favorites list, but that is the ultimate goal. It might involve going back to the first stage and wishing happiness and forgiveness for yourself, then trying again at a later date.

If you are interested in the loving-kindness meditation, a great place to start is with the YouTube video by Sharon Salzburg. It's called Guided Meditation by Sharon Salzburg. You can also take a look at the book Loving-Kindness, by Sharon Salzberg.

Key Takeaway Points From Chapter 8

- **A mentor or teacher can help with your meditation practice, both with keeping up the motivation when you feel "stuck" and to learn about specific traditions and techniques.**

- Object Focused Meditation uses an external object to focus the mind, such as a flower, candle flame, etc.
- Visualization meditations involve getting the mind's eye to see and feel events, places, and objects. This is quite different from attention focused meditations and has specific goals. An example would be an athlete that is visualizing the exact moves required to pull off a ski run or golf shot, attempting to build a mental pathway in the brain that will help him or her succeed when they attempt the real-world actions. Other visualizations may be designed to relax you, etc.
- Mantras are repeated words or phrases used to focus your mind and slow down or redirect thoughts.
- Transcendental meditation is a trademarked meditation brand that is practiced worldwide. It seems highly effective at reducing stress and depression, and its practitioners are extremely supportive of it.

- **Loving-Kindness Meditation focuses on creating feelings of compassion, wellbeing, and happiness for yourself and others.**

CHAPTER 9

WHERE TO GO FROM HERE

Keep Up The Practice!

A 90-day Meditation Challenge is all well and good, but where does this leave you at the end of it? Is it over and done with, water under the bridge, next thing on the agenda?

Hopefully, this is just the beginning for your quest of self-discovery. After completing this challenge, you will have only scratched the surface of what daily meditation practice is all about.

If you succeeded in focusing on the good feelings that meditation brings about in the body, you will have lots of reasons to continue and will want to have the feelings of positivity and joy that you have started experiencing. The best news is, with continued practice, these feelings can eventually become a default position for you. It will overflow into every area as you mindfully notice small pleasures you previously missed entirely. From how a soft fabric feels against your body to the warmth of your coffee cup in your hand, these experiences were always there, just inaccessible to your conscious mind.

To reach that stage, you will need to keep up the practice. The best way to make sure that happens is to plan ahead for how you intend your life to unfold, with meditation as a part of it. Here are a few ways you can enrich your meditation practice and maybe even take it to the next level.

Joining a Monastery

Really the only option at this point is becoming a monk in a monastery. You will need to sell all of your belongings and donate the proceeds to feeding the rich, shave your head and get some very uncomfortable robes. These robes should preferably be made from wool or old rags and have a very bland color. Footwear will need to be sandals or flip flops, Crocs being the only exception to this.

Now that you are outfitted properly, you can apply to monasteries in foreign countries where they don't speak the same language as you, and hopefully, they will take you in since you are now destitute, a homeless person. This might take several attempts as they make you wait outside on the street for several days to prove you're really interested in coming inside. Don't be discouraged, even if the small street children and feral dogs steal what little you have left while you sleep on the sidewalk.

Eventually, the monks will have to let you in and hear you out. Make sure you express your dedication, mentioning that you managed to make it through a 90-Day Meditation Challenge. This should qualify you for a spot with them. They will give you a small stone cubicle to live in and a mattress stuffed with straw. Shared outdoor "bathrooms" will also be provided.

You will have plenty of time to continue practicing your meditations in your spare time after working the fields with your bare hands each day. Food will be edible, but not interesting. And the Wi-Fi will be terrible. The biggest advantage of living here is being totally cut off from politics and daily news, which will increase your chances of happiness significantly.

Alternatively, you can try some of these other options. They won't be as effective, however. Joining a monastery is a tried and true method of every movie we can think of. Look what happened for Doctor Strange, not only did he end up with a really cool cloak, but he eventually left the monastery and got to travel to other planets and stuff.

Workshops, Courses, and Local Meditation Groups

We mentioned before that finding a mentor or teacher could really benefit the meditation practice. A great place to start would be with a meditation workshop or weekend course. These are held in every city and are advertised locally as well as online. This would be a great way to try out different meditation techniques to find out what will work best for you.

There's a good chance that there is a group of people in your area who meet regularly to meditate and share communally. Joining a group like this has the effect of bolstering your dedication to your daily practice, reinforcing your desire to sit daily. Group meditation can also be more profound, a deeper experience that is shared by a like-minded group. It has to be experienced to be understood!

You can find a group on sites like meetup.com or Facebook. If there isn't a mindfulness or meditation group near you, consider starting one.

Meditation Retreats

Meditation retreats are a great way to deepen your practice and go beyond what you can read from a book. You may have heard about retreats and wondered if they are for you. There are many different types, from free retreats staffed by volunteers to destination meditation retreats at resorts in exotic places. Let's take a look at some of the reasons you might want to sign up for one.

The most obvious benefit to a meditation retreat is focus. The intent behind a retreat is to get away from all the distractions of the regular day to day and focus on things such as learning a specific technique, or nature, etc. Many retreats are secluded and surrounded by forest, which gives an excellent chance to reconnect with the natural world. Electronic devices such as cell phones may be against the rules. Talking may be limited or even avoided entirely for the duration of the retreat.

One effect of holding a meditation retreat is to gather like-minded individuals in one place, resulting in a positive and supportive environment. The intent is to be happy and at peace. This will increase the benefits to the participants and aid them with their practice.

Teachers and mentorship are a big benefit of retreats as well. There will be expert guidance on hand. These people are experienced and trained meditators that can address concerns, coach you in specific techniques, and give you feedback.

At most retreats, your day-to-day needs will be taken care of so that you can relax and pay attention to your practice. Food will be prepared, and everything organized for you, eliminating stress about meals and cleanup.

Retreats vary in length from one day to weeks. If you're unsure about a long retreat or simply can't get away for a week, then a weekend-long retreat may fit your needs the best. This would allow you to see what a retreat would be like before committing to a longer one.

Going on a retreat can be considered an act of self-care, where your personal growth and wellbeing are at the forefront. It is a choice to focus on yourself and get away, and this makes it possible to see the world from an entirely new perspective. With a retreat that lasts more than a few days, this change in perspective makes personal change more likely. You aren't locked into your regular, rigid worldview, you are in a neutral place, able to know a different side.

While it's possible to spend money to go on a destination retreat, for those with budget limitations, there are free and donation-based retreats. An example of this is the Vipassana Meditation, retreats that can be found worldwide. The site www.dhamma.org has more details about these retreats, which take the form of 10-day courses. The meditation technique is taught over the 10 days, with food and lodging provided, and volunteers preparing meals, etc. There are 12 centers in the US and 5 in Canada, and many more in other countries, making it accessible to almost anyone who can find 10 days to attend.

Vipassana means to see things as they really are, and the techniques are focused on the body and awareness, while silence is observed. There is no talking between students. The participants are allowed to talk to the teacher, and to the staff concerning material needs. This type of retreat is hard work and requires a serious time commitment, but it has long term benefits that can only be gained through attending.

Set Up Your Own Mini-Meditation Retreat

Is a regular retreat out of your reach right now? All is not lost. Just because you can't afford the time or money to go on an organized meditation retreat doesn't mean you can't stage your own mini-retreat. All you need is a few hours to a couple days you can either get away or make everyone else get away. This could be a Sunday morning or the entire weekend, or even that Thursday you are going to be getting off work. Another advantage to trying your own mini-retreat is that you will know if you are still interested in one of the longer, organized-for-you versions.

If you can line up a day to yourself at home and find a way to keep your family/ roommates/ significant other(s) out of the picture for the duration, then this could be your mini-retreat. Set your ground rules for the time period, lock the door and begin.

To maximize your experience, put a little thought into your retreat. Think about your intention for this time, what you want to get out of the experience, and write it down. You might come up with something like "My Sunday meditation retreat will be a stress detox and a way to get ready for the busy week ahead!"

Schedule the time and put it into your calendar. Treat this just like an appointment that you've already paid good money for, and therefore, nothing will stop you from showing up to get your money's worth! Decide ahead of time what you will be doing on your retreat. This could be a specific practice you want to try or some yoga, etc. Just like in beginning our 90-day Meditation Challenge, we want to make this as convenient as possible, so you have very few decisions to make during the retreat.

Type up or write out your schedule so you can hang it up or put it out for you to refer to. How about a quick sample schedule?

08:00 - Morning meditation
08:30 - light breakfast - yogurt, orange
09:00 - Yoga with Adriene – video on YouTube

09:30 - Green Tea Break! (or another hot beverage)
10:00 - Walking meditation - back yard
10:30 - inspirational reading, journaling
12:00 - Lunch - healthy foods and more green tea
1:00 - Guided visualization, or sitting meditation
2:00 - Inspirational Reading
3:00 - Walking meditation followed by sitting meditation
3:45 - Green tea
4:00 - welcome the family home

Sample retreat rules:

- Put the cellphone on "do not disturb"
- Shut off Netflix, and if possible, disable the wifi! (except while watching the yoga video)
- Wear comfortable (or no) clothing as you see fit - except for the walking meditation if you leave the house
- Have a healthy, renewing snack and lunch planned and pre-made

Another great mini-retreat idea is to go to a place in nature and find a good place to meditate there. This could be a quiet park, a secluded beach, or a small forested area. Make sure you bring the right gear, such as:

- Bug spray
- Sunscreen
- Warm sweater (if it's chilly)
- Yoga mat, blanket, or pillow
- An inspirational book to read before or after your meditation session

So you see, it's possible to go on a meditation retreat without spending money, even if you can only find a day to fit it in. These solo journeys can, in some ways, act as a silent meditation retreat depending on how you go about it. It would be best to limit electronic device time and avoid communication with your best buds by text unless it's an emergency. Going on your mini-retreat and just spending the time on Instagram, then messaging everyone on Facebook, isn't going to have nearly the same effect as spending this time in reflection.

These personal retreats can become a way to get in your self-care, a way to recharge and de-stress from all of the demands put on you day to day. If you try one out and it goes well, consider making it a personal ritual that you repeat on a regular basis.

Kyla's Silent Retreat Experience

You wanna know how crazy you are? Be silent.

Our minds are so quick to form an opinion, and the urge to share that opinion is an urge purely of ego. We wish to share our perspective, and many times we have the answer readily available before the other person has even finished a sentence. The reasons vary, perhaps our minds wish to defend against the offerings of another's mind, simply because it challenges us to a personal belief we hold as true. Or it can be a compulsion to make noise, so we don't have to really pay attention to the whispers of the heart. This compulsion can become so strong to make noise that we will even hold conversations with ourselves. When we make the conscious choice to be silent, it is here, we get a glimpse into the thoughts we are having and the feelings we are ignoring. There is some truth to the statement that silence is golden.

The longest time I have personally spent in silence is five days. It was not a silent guided retreat, I had decided to do it on my own, after seeing it mentioned in a few books on meditation, and the results surprised me. I didn't go to work as usual, and my son was very young, so I waited until I had some time on my own. I had been reading about the practice of silence in reference to monitoring the thoughts of the mind and to truly "hear" what is coming from my mind. It was amazing to see how quickly I spoke, even the impulse to talk to myself was very strong. I was amazed at how much my mind wanted to engage with life. I was almost a decade into my meditation practice, and I had thought that silence would be easy. The first day was by far the most challenging, it was fascinating to see how much I wanted to talk, or just to make noise. As time went on and I focused more and more on the impulses, the things I wanted to say, I became aware of a few things. The first was how my knee-jerk reaction to speak was just mind or my ego wanting to assess the situation, give it a label or opinion, and I would watch the impulse go and have the opportunity to see the beliefs I was holding that I couldn't really see before. The second was, after a bit of time, I began to hear my heart. I would just sit there and would see something, and because I could not react verbally, my only choice was to enjoy it as it was. I think, for the first time, I really appreciated that this experience, this life was truly unique to my perspective. If something upset me emotionally, I was able to see it more for what it was, I was forced, instead of verbalizing my discontent, to sit with it. I was fascinated to find how, without the opportunity to verbalize my discontent, without the opportunity to generate an entire verbal story around one fleeting moment, how quickly it would pass. I also learned how much more I could hear. Silence connected me more deeply to the sounds that surrounded me, the sounds of nature. When someone would speak, I would hear them, not just their words but the feelings behind them. In silence, I learned to hear. I learned to hear my heart.

Great Books That Can Help Your Practice

> *"Someone asked me, If I were stranded on a desert island, what book I would bring... 'How to Build a Boat.'"*
> *-Steven Wright*

Books can help in so many ways. Firstly, you can get helpful descriptions and guides for specific techniques you can try, along with guidance from experienced meditators that you might never be able to meet in real life. Books are like a window into the minds of some of the world's most knowledgeable and helpful teachers and mentors, and this is an invaluable resource. But as helpful as this is, there is an even more important role that a good book will have for most people. They are motivation in a portable bundle, encouragement between two covers, a reminder to stay on the path you chose to set out on. When you lose sight of your goal, reading a few pages of the right manuscript will help you get back on target. When you get discouraged or lose hope from what seems like slow progress and setbacks, you can be re-inspired by an author's passionate descriptions.

This is why it can be so helpful and important to locate the author that speaks the best to you. Each person will have their individual needs and will want to find a book that speaks to their heart. Here are some of the ones that speak to us. There are so many good books out there that we haven't had time to read them all so you will be able to find many more out there that are excellent.

Loving-Kindness, by Sharon Salzberg
The Miracle of Mindfulness, by Thich Nhat Hanh
How to Meditate, by Pema Chodron
Meditation for Beginners, by Jack Kornfield
Peace Is Every Step: The Path of Mindfulness in Everyday Life, by Thich Nhat Hanh
The Power of Now: A Guide To Spiritual Enlightenment, by Eckhart Tolle
The Mind Illuminated: A Complete Meditation Guide, by Culadas (John Yates, Ph.D.)
Radical Acceptance: Embracing Your Life With The Heart of a Buddha, by Tara Brach
Silence: The power of quiet in a world full of noise, by Thich Nhat Hanh

Resources

Here are a few links and other resources that you might want to take a look at.

Tim-Ebl.com - that's right! Tim has his own website, so he can put all kinds of crazy stuff in there, and no one can stop him! (Cue evil villain laugh)

Apart from information about this and upcoming books that are in the works, you can find a link to download those free gifts that we really, really, really want you to have. There will also be a contact form there to ask us any questions and information about contests and events. Please come check out Tim-Ebl.com

90-Day Meditation Challenge Facebook Page - we already talked about this, but it is a resource, so we will also mention it again here- drop by and take a look- www.facebook.com/groups/90DayMeditationChallenge/

www.intothewildwithkyla.com - Kyla has lots of great content on her site

Instagram: @mindful_tim_ebl

Key Takeaway Points From Chapter 9

- **Monasteries are the ultimate way to increase your meditation cred, but they aren't for everyone**
- **Instead, you can most likely find local meditation groups that host gatherings on weekends or evenings**

- Meditation retreats are a popular and highly recommended way to deepen your practice
- Holding your own mini-retreat is the most practical option for some, requiring a few hours minimum and a quiet location
- Silent retreats are not for the faint of heart! Be sure you are up to the challenge
- If you haven't located a teacher, group, or workshop, there are many great books available

CHAPTER 10

CONCLUSION

> *"If every eight-year-old in the world is taught meditation, we will eliminate violence from the world in one generation."*
> -Dali Lama

What we Hope For You

When we started this journey with you, we hoped to inspire you to start meditating daily and build a lifelong habit of self-care and mental training. We hope that you are still working your way toward the end of the 90-day challenge, even though the book is ending! And we hope you will keep going, keep learning, sending ripples of positive change through your life out into the world.

Wouldn't it be nice if your meditation caused a chain reaction that saved the entire universe? Let's just sit back and enjoy that thought! What if, because you started a regular meditation practice, you subtly altered your outlook and became just a little more forgiving, a little more patient. Because of this, you raised a daughter that is just a bit happier and more playful, and she took that with her to school. She had a parent who didn't yell as much and had a lot deeper connection with her, so because of this, she was secure in herself. So when the other kids started bullying this little boy, Justin, she stood up for him, and he didn't feel so lonely. He didn't have as much pain in his heart, so he wasn't attracted to videos on YouTube featuring horrible acts of real violence. He didn't join a chat-group based around white supremacy, and he never ended up deciding to, one day, take his father's pistol to school.

Because of this, he never shot three of his classmates on February third, 2029, and he didn't kill the girl who was fated to go on to university to study carbon capture technology. So since this girl, who now lived, was able to get through university and get hired by a climate-saving startup, she developed a revolutionary process that removes carbon and pollutants directly from the air while creating nearly free energy, as well as a meat substitute that actually tastes like meat!

These inventions save the human race and millions of animals. We then go on to save the entire universe, but that's a story for another day.

Our point is, you can't tell how far-reaching the events of your day-to-day life truly are. A lot of the focus on meditation only looks at the effects on the person doing the practice, how it affects their mind, soul, and body. But what about all the effects on their surroundings? What does it do for the world when a person becomes more mindful, less reactionary, more emotionally stable? How does this affect workplaces, families, and public transit? We don't exist in a bubble; we are all co-dependent on this planet.

You may have heard of the six degrees of separation, which is the theory that all people on Earth are only six or less social connections away from each other. That means that you are a friend of a friend of a friend of someone who knows Kevin Bacon's hair stylist, or maybe less of a chain of people. By this theory, learning to be a proficient meditator could potentially affect the life of anyone in some way, even that of Kevin Bacon! Your upgraded brain could send that ripple that does indeed make a difference.

So before you take a seat on that meditation cushion, remember that this isn't all about you. It's about your friends, your children if you have any, your boss (or employees), and all the others that you interact with. It's about the choices you make as you become more mindful and decide to stop supporting a company with questionable environmental practices, that previously, you never paid attention to. It's about learning mental skills that lead to a better relationship with your husband, which ends up meaning your marriage lasts for 40 more years. It's about you, too, but you go out and spread your you-ness to all these other people. Meditation can help you be the very best version of yourself.

And that is where we will say goodbye, with our hope that we have helped you, even a little, to become your true self.

ACKNOWLEDGMENTS

Kyla –

- Thank you to Ty and Seth, you have taught me the true meaning of love.
- Doran, Thank you for being you my love, and for loving me as I am.
- Thank you to my family and friends both here and gone.
- Thank you to my teachers and students, you are one and the same.

Tim -

- My wife, Nicole, who has put up with me sitting around for hours in silence, ignoring her to focus on my own inner needs. She has never complained when I sat with my eyes closed in public,

obviously doing something weird and embarrassing like meditating at the airport. Thanks for supporting me, honey.
- My daughter Bethany, who loves books so much it scares me and is an awesome makeup artist
- My son Andrew, who always insists on seeing the world positively, even when he shouldn't, and manages to come out on top
- My son Eric, who bravely went where no Ebl has gone before, then returned, then decided he wanted to go back - thanks for following your dreams and not settling
- Dan Papanek and Roxanne Dearing - because of their feedback and support, I got off my butt and finished this book
- Happy Self Publishing, for all of your excellent work on the cover, editing and coordination
- Amazon, for making it possible for independent authors to get their books out into the light of day
- Self Publishing School, for giving me the inspiration and tools to become an author

Thank you for reading!
We are honored that you spent this time with us.

We would love it if you could help us by leaving your honest review at amazon.com. We want to be able to reach as many people as possible with our message, to try to make the world a better place for everyone. Your honesty and input will help our book get to the people that need it!

Please Pay It Forward!

Give us a quick review and let us know what you loved about our book! We are eternally grateful for all those who take two minutes to leave their feedback.

Made in the USA
Lexington, KY
29 June 2019